ACQUIRING SKILL IN SPORT

Whether it's a gymnast balancing perfectly on a beam, a rugby player receiving a pass whilst sprinting for the line, or a swimmer stroking smoothly through the water, success in sport depends on well learned movement skills.

Acquiring Skill in Sport guides you through the science that underlies these skills, using practical examples to explain the concepts discussed. It covers:

▪ The characteristics and classification of skills and abilities in sport
▪ Theories of skill learning and motor control
▪ Individual differences and phases of skill learning
▪ Approaches to effective guidance and teaching of sport skills

Clearly written and illustrated throughout, with questions to test knowledge and understanding, this is an ideal introductory text for students of physical education, sport, human movement science and kinesiology, as well as coaches seeking to develop their understanding of sports skills.

John Honeybourne is a freelance Education Consultant with more than twenty-seven years' experience teaching physical education. He is an A Level Principal Examiner for a major examination board and an Ofsted Inspector for physical education. He is also the author of a range of textbooks, study materials and revision guides for physical education and sport.

STUDENT SPORT STUDIES
Series Editors: J. A. Mangan and Frank Galligan

This is a new series specifically for school, college and university students, written clearly and concisely by expert teachers. The series covers a range of relevant topics for those studying physical education, sports studies, leisure and recreation studies and related courses. Each volume is purposefully prepared for students facing specific course syllabuses and examinations and is sharply focused and written in plain English. The series is in response to repeated requests from students and teachers for accessible books concentrating on courses and examinations.

J. A. Mangan
Frank Galligan
2004

Other titles in the series

The Story of English Sport
Neil Wigglesworth

In Pursuit of Excellence
A Contemporary Issue
Michael Hill

The Olympic Games Explained
A Student Guide to the Evolution of the Modern Olympic Games
Vassil Girginov and Jim Parry

ACQUIRING SKILL IN SPORT

An Introduction

JOHN HONEYBOURNE

Routledge
Taylor & Francis Group

LONDON AND NEW YORK

First published 2006 by Routledge
2 Park Square, Milton Park, Abingdon, Oxon OX14 4RN

Simultaneously published in the USA and Canada
by Taylor & Francis Inc
270 Madison Avenue, New York, NY 10016

Routledge is an imprint of the Taylor & Francis Group, an informa business

© 2006 John Honeybourne

Typeset in Mixage by Keystroke, 28 High Street, Tettenhall, Wolverhampton
Printed and bound in Great Britain by MPG Books Ltd, Bodmin

Every effort has been made to ensure that the advice and information
in this book is true and accurate at the time of going to press. However,
neither the publisher nor the authors can accept any legal responsibility
or liability for any errors or omissions that may be made.

British Library Cataloguing in Publication Data
A catalogue record for this book is available from the British Library

Library of Congress Cataloging in Publication Data
Honeybourne, John.
Acquiring skill in sport / John Honeybourne.
p. cm. – (Student sport studies)
Includes bibliographical references and index.
ISBN 0–415–34935–4 (hardback) – ISBN 0–415–34936–2 (pbk.)
1. Physical education and training–Study and teaching. I. Title.
II. Series.
GV361.H585 2006
613.7071–dc22   2006002922

ISBN10: 0–415–34935–4 (hbk)
ISBN10: 0–415–34936–2 (pbk)
ISBN10: 0–203–00482–5 (ebk)

ISBN13: 978–0–415–34935–2 (hbk)
ISBN13: 978–0–415–34936–9 (pbk)
ISBN13: 978–0–203–00482–1 (ebk)

CONTENTS

LIST OF ILLUSTRATIONS

Plates

Figures

INTRODUCTION

This easy-to-follow textbook is designed to help in developing an understanding of the basic concepts related to the acquisition of motor skills in sport.

The book is particularly relevant to students and teachers of *all* A/S, A2 level and BTEC sports-related courses, as well as those coaches who need to develop an understanding of the theoretical elements within coaching courses.

Whatever the examination board or awarding body, this textbook will cover the main areas of study within the subject field.

Courses often include modules or sections dedicated to the acquisition of motor skills. This textbook is the first of its kind to be written specifically for students and is intended to cover the field of study in greater depth than is possible within the page limitations of more wide-ranging texts.

The depth of analysis and ease of reading also make this text suitable for sport/physical education undergraduates and for teachers – especially those with little or no background in the subject field or who may be revisiting it for the first time in a number of years!

Each chapter covers the relevant research into that area of study and applies it to practical sports examples. There are separate boxes on many pages with appropriate examples related to a sporting context.

For a full understanding it is important to define the technical terms that are used in skill acquisition and these are widely used and defined within each chapter.

As an aid to test understanding and to assist with any revision there are a number of questions at the end of each chapter.

Other texts referred to by the author and suggested as further reading are also listed at the end of each chapter.

Advanced and degree courses in physical education, sports studies and sports science often include the subject area of motor skill acquisition. This area of study is really a part of sports psychology because it involves human learning.

This text covers the subject by dealing initially with skill(s) and then the theories related to the learning of those skills. Finally, the ways in which skills can be taught to those who wish to learn and/or improve them are dealt with.

In Chapters 1 and 2 the nature of skill and ability is explored along with any similarities and important differences. Systems of skill classification are also covered in these chapters and this enables the student of skill acquisition to analyse the requirements of motor skill tasks and enables coaches to focus on aspects of a skill in order to optimise learning.

Chapters 3 and 4 cover the cybernetic view of skill learning and explore in detail the theory of *information processing*, which incorporates the mechanisms of perception and memory. The concept of motor control is also covered and this explains the important stages of the motor skill learning process.

Chapter 5 investigates the differences between individual performers and how this is applied to the way in which motor skills are learned and performed. The individual must be motivated in order to learn motor skills successfully and this chapter examines the different forms and levels of motivation.

Levels of anxiety and type of personality also vary from one individual to another and this chapter explores the nature of personality, how it can affect skill learning and how this may lead to modifications in the way that sports skills are taught.

Chapter 6 takes a straightforward but comprehensive look at learning theories. This is a fascinating area of study but the reader is steered through the complexities of each theory with clear explanations and relevant practical examples. There are many learning theories but this text concentrates on those most likely to be the subject of examination board specifications and modular papers.

A number of methods are employed in the teaching and coaching of motor skills but it is important to adopt the most appropriate method in order to ensure effective learning.

Chapters 7, 8 and 9 cover the theories and practical advice that will lead to effective and efficient teaching and coaching of sports skills.

Chapter 7 looks specifically at the sequence of learning phases that we pass through as we learn and subsequently improve motor skills. These patterns of learning are often visually expressed in the form of learning curves.

Chapter 8 addresses the ways in which we can manipulate both skills and practices to ensure the most effective learning environment.

Chapter 9 looks at the styles of teaching that can be employed and which can be adopted and adapted depending on the nature of the task, the ability level of the performer and the environmental circumstances.

As you read each section of the text, always put the theoretical principles into a practical context – there are examples given to help you. Remember, practice does not make perfect but perfect practice can make you a darn sight better!

Good teaching and coaching are both built on the sound theoretical principles that come from sound research. This text will take you on a journey through the research and the theory in order to help you to help sporting individuals to realise their potential – good luck!

chapter one

CHARACTERISTICS AND CLASSIFICATION OF SKILLS IN SPORT

the learned ability to bring about predetermined results with maximum certainty often with the minimum outlay of time or energy or both.

Knapp (1963)

Characteristics of skill and skilful performance

The word *skill* is often used in sport and can be used to describe movements such as dribbling a football. However, the word *skilful* is used to describe the motor movements of someone who has achieved excellence in their activity.

A sports performer who is deemed to be skilful often possesses the qualities of co-ordination, fluency, control, economy and efficiency of movement. Skills in sport when fully learned have an aesthetic quality because of the fluidity of the movement shown. Even professional boxers demonstrate a beauty of movement because of the speed and flow of technically accurate motor skills related to footwork and combinations of punches.

Skills that are fully learned are pre-planned and are directed towards a pre-determined goal. For example, a skilful netball player will have worked out a plan of movement – often called a motor plan. This motor plan will have been formulated by referring to previous experiences of using that particular skill or movement that are held in the long-term memory.

All preparatory movements and subsequent execution of that skill would then be directed towards fulfilling the aims planned by the performer.

The following is another well known definition of skill:

An organised coordinated activity in relation to an object or a situation which involves a whole chain of sensory, central and motor mechanisms

> . . . the performance is continuously under the control of the sensory input . . . which controls the performance in the sense that outcomes of actions are continuously matched against some criterion of achievements or degree of approach to a goal according to which the performance is corrected.
>
> **Argyle and Kendon (1967)**

There are three main types of skill in sport: (1) cognitive skills, (2) perceptual skills, (3) fundamental motor skills.

Cognitive skills

These are the intellectual/mental skills of the sports performer. These skills affect perception. They are essential for effective decision-making and problem solving.

In order to perform skills, we need certain underlying factors such as strength and hand–eye co-ordination. These factors are known as abilities and are different from skills. This is because abilities are largely determined genetically; in other words they are naturally occurring and enduring characteristics. Skills, on the other hand, are learned through practice.

EXAMPLE

A rugby player makes the decision to kick rather than pass in a 'pressure situation'. This decision is based on a cognitive assessment.

Perceptual skills

These involve the interpretation of information received so that a motor plan can be formulated. Perception is affected by previous experiences and attentional control.

A slalom skier assesses the timing of a turn by taking into account (perceiving) his own position and the position of the gate in relation to his downhill speed.

PLATE 1 Perception of space and speed can critically affect timing

Photo: Tony Marshall/EmPics Sports Photo Agency

Skills that require a great deal of interpretation of the sensory input are known as *complex skills*. Skills that do not have many perceptual demands are known as *simple skills*.

Motor skills

These are physical limb movements that are directed towards the achievement of a particular goal.

Fundamental motor skills

These are basic skills learned at a young age, usually through play. If learned thoroughly, they can be adapted or refined to form all or part of specific sports skills.

PLATE 2 Fundamental motor skills can be combined to produce advanced/ complex skills

Photo: Lucy Nicholson/AP/EmPics Sports Photo Agency

The skills we use in sports are sophisticated versions of these fundamental motor skills. The overarm throw is part of many sports movements, as for example, those found in cricket, tennis and the javelin throw.

It is thought that when children acquire motor skills, they acquire these fundamental skills at a first or primary level and that these skills are built upon through trial and error, experience and through additional learned movements.

In the early years at school – from reception class to year 3 – children should be given lots of opportunities to develop fundamental motor skills such as those involving kicking, striking, catching and vertical jumping. Once these skills are thoroughly learned then skills that are more 'sports-specific' can be developed.

Figure 1 shows the effects of the learning of fundamental motor skills on the performance of specific sports skills.

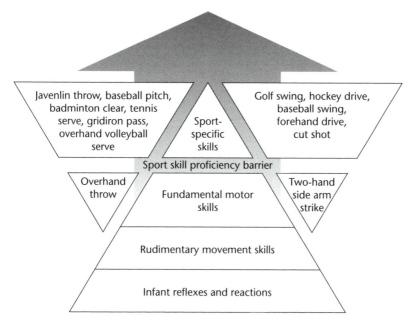

FIGURE 1 Effects of fundamental motor skills on the performance of sport-specific skills (Department of Education, Victoria, 1996)

The classification of skills in sport

The process of classifying skills is not an exact science because of the complex nature of motor skills. Classification does, however, help to provide a useful analysis of the nature of different types of skills used in sport. If the nature of skills is understood more fully then it is more likely that effective teaching and learning will take place, and with this greater understanding teachers and coaches can adapt both their methods and the teaching/learning environment in order to maximise the learning of skills.

The systems used to classify sports skills are normally bi-polar and should be viewed as continua. Although some sports skills are referred to as 'closed', no skill in sport is completely closed; there are always *some* environmental influences. A basketball player taking a free shot may do so in an environment where the distance and the position of the hoop are fixed but there are other aspects of the environment that are variable and which may affect the skill being performed. The presence of other players and spectators, for example, may affect the execution of the skill, however well rehearsed it might be.

Classification is a process of categorising skills that share characteristics. It is therefore a general approach and should be viewed as such.

Open/closed classification

This method of classifying skills centres on the effects of the surrounding environment on the execution of that skill. It is based on the work of Poulton (1957), who investigated the classification of motor skills in an industrial setting. In this classification 'the environment' includes other sports performers that may be involved.

The system states that if a skill is affected by the surrounding environment and requires the performer to make perceptual decisions/adjustments, it is called an *open* skill. Conversely, if a skill is not affected at all by the environment in which it is performed then it is referred to as a *closed* skill.

This classification scale is also often referred to as 'the open/closed continuum'.

In the above and other similar situations (e.g. rugby or hockey) the environment is referred to almost constantly by the player who is about to make the tackle.

Open skills   **Closed skills**

Football tackle   Basketball free throw

FIGURE 2 Classifying skills: the open–closed continuum

Features of open skills:

- Environment is unpredictable, therefore adaptation is necessary.
- Many perceptual requirements.
- No definite beginning or end to the skill.
- Predominantly externally paced.

Features of closed skills:

- Environment mainly constant, therefore few adaptations are necessary.
- Predominantly habitual.
- Normally a definite beginning and end to the skill.
- Predominantly self-paced.

Timing/pacing of skills

The timing or *pacing* aspects of skills are also included in the classification of open and closed skills. When a skill is said to be predominantly *self-paced*, the performer has most of the control over the speed at which the skill is performed. Conversely, when a skill is referred to as being predominantly 'externally paced', external influences control the speed at which the skill is performed.

The more a sports performer is proactive in skill production the more self-paced the skill. If the performer reacts or responds to external stimuli then normally the skill will be referred to as externally paced.

Skills towards the closed end of the open/closed continuum tend to be more self-paced. Skills that are more open in nature will usually be more externally paced.

EXAMPLE

The pole vault is a skill that would be placed towards the 'closed' end of the open/closed continuum because the external environment is stable and has little effect on the execution of the skill. There are no direct opponents to interfere with the execution of the skill.

The pole vault, like, say, a discus throw is also predominantly 'self-paced'. The speed of the vault or the throw is determined almost completely by the thrower – who does not have to react to external stimuli or overcome an opponent in order to perform the skill.

Gentile *et al.* (1975) proposed a four-category system of classification that is sport-specific. The categories are:

- *Stationary/no change:* responding to a motionless object and there is no change in response requirements over time.

PLATE 3 A 'closed skill' is subject to little outside interference and will not normally require adjustment during performance

Photo: Photodisk

- *In motion/no change:* responding to an object that is moving and there is no change in response requirements over time.
- *Stationary/change:* responding to a motionless object and the response requirements change from one response to the next.
- *In motion/change:* responding to an object that is moving and the response requirements change from one response to the next.

This four-category system can be used to identify which skills can be modified for teaching purposes. Magill (1993) has given an example of an instruction sequence for learning to hit a ball thrown by a pitcher in baseball (see Figure 3).

Stationary/ No change (Closed skills)	Stationary/ Change	In motion/ No change	In motion/ Change (Open skills)
(Category 1) Batting a stationary ball from a tee	(Category 2) Batting a ball from a tee that changes height	(Category 3) Batting a ball from a pitching machine	(Category 4) Batting a ball from a live pitcher

FIGURE 3 A four-category system of classification (Magill 1993)

Gross and fine motor skills

Another method of classifying skills is based on an analysing that focuses on how precise the associated movements are. Again the classification should be viewed on a continuum between the two extremes of gross movements and fine movements.

Skills towards the gross end of this continuum involve large muscle movements and precision is not a feature of skill production. Earlier in this chapter we explored the nature of fundamental motor skills and these are predominantly categorised as gross skills – such as running and jumping.

Fine motor skills are those that are concerned with precise movements. There is normally a great deal of eye–hand co-ordination and 'steady control' involved in such skills.

EXAMPLE

A snooker shot involves small or 'fine' movements, as do many other 'aiming' activities.

This is a straightforward classification but it has been useful in the analysis of movement, particularly in rehabilitation following a sporting injury. In many situations skills are performed with both gross and fine actions: a bowler in cricket can perform gross movements in the run-up but may use very fine movements to achieve a spin on the ball (see Figure 4).

acquiring skill in sport

Gross skills	**Fine skills**
Bowling in cricket	Snooker
(run-up)	shot

FIGURE 4 Gross–fine skills continuum

PLATE 4 The tiniest movements are critical here

Photo: Adam Davy/EmPics Sports Photo Agency

Discrete, serial and continuous skills

Discrete skills

Skills that have a definite beginning and end are called discrete skills, for example kicking a ball. The start and finishing points must be adhered to if there is to be successful performance of the skill.

Discrete skills are often linked, which makes them serial skills; in other words a small collection of separate skills put into one, for example a gymnastic floor routine.

Skills that have elements that are very difficult to separate out are referred to as *continuous* skills, for example the leg action in the front-crawl swimming stroke.

This type of classification is important to understanding the control of movement in sport and whether a skill can be broken into its constituent parts for more effective skill learning.

EXAMPLE

A discrete skill such as a penalty hit in hockey has a definite start and end. The learner must be able to visualise the start and finish so that they can be copied.

Serial skills

A serial skill can be split into discrete parts such as the triple jump in athletics. Each element can then be taught separately and then re-linked in order to produce the complete skill.

Continuous skills

Continuous skills such as the leg action in cycling must be practised as a whole to retain the fluidity of movement; the use of stabilisers on a bicycle is therefore a good way for the young learner to practise the leg action in safety.

Implications for training and coaching

If a closed skill is to be coached, then it is going to be more effective if it is practised repetitively so that the skill becomes 'grooved'. It is often not necessary to vary the way in which it is practised because closed skills remain largely constant.

Conversely, when coaching or teaching open skills a variety of situations must be created in order to allow the performer to build up a repertoire of strategies to cope with a range of fast-changing scenarios in which the skill may need to be performed.

Discrete skills are probably most effectively taught as 'whole skills' although at an advanced level there may be some advantage in breaking them down in order to address specific points or difficulties.

Conversely, serial skills are often more effectively taught by breaking them down into a series of 'sub-routines' or 'parts'. Each part can be taught/learned in isolation before the skill is practised as a whole entity.

It is difficult to split continuous skills into parts or sub-routines without adversely affecting the 'flow' of the skill. It is therefore probably more effective to practise such skills as a whole so that the kinaesthetic sense of the movement is not lost.

CHARACTERISTICS AND CLASSIFICATION OF SKILLS IN SPORT

1. (a) Are you able to define the words 'skill' and 'skilful' in the context of sport?
   (b) Can you describe the main characteristics of skilful movement, using sporting examples?

2. Can you define and give examples of:

   (a) cognitive skills
   (b) perceptual skills
   (c) motor skills
   (d) fundamental motor skills

3. Why is the use of a classification of skills so important to those who are teaching and learning motor skills in sport?

4. Can you draw an open/closed continuum and place the following skills on it:

   (a) long jump
   (b) rugby tackle
   (c) volleyball dig
   (d) basketball dribble

5. What are the main features of closed skills?

6. What is meant when a skill is referred to as being 'externally paced'? Give an example of such a skill from sport.

7. Explain Gentile's four-category open/closed model of skill classification in sport.

8 Using examples from sport explain the differences between gross skills and fine skills.
9 How does the teaching /coaching of 'discrete skills' differ from that of 'continuous skills' in sport?
10 Could you provide some practical tips to a coach in a specific sport about the teaching of skills related to skill classification.

Texts referred to in this chapter

Argyle, M and Kendon, A. 'The experimental analysis of social performance', in L. Berkowitz (ed.) *Advances in experimental social psychology*, Vol. III. New York, Academic Press, 1967.

Department of Education, Victoria. *Fundamental Motor Skills: a Classroom Manual for Teachers*, Melbourne, Community Information Service, Department of Education, Victoria, 1996.

Gentile, A. M., Higgins, J. R., Miller, E. A., and Rosen, B. M. 'The structure of motor tasks', *Mouvement*, 7, 11–28, 1975.

Honeybourne J. *BTEC National Sport*, Cheltenham, Nelson Thornes, 2003.

Knapp, B. *Skill in Sport*, London, Routledge & Kegan Paul, 1963.

Magill, R. A. *Motor Learning Concepts and Applications*, Guilford CT: Brown and Benchmark, 1993.

Poulton, E. C. 'On prediction in skilled movements', *Psychological Bulletin*, 54, 467–78, 1957.

chapter two

CHARACTERISTICS AND CLASSIFICATION OF ABILITIES IN SPORT

There has been much discussion about the differences between the terms 'ability' and 'skill'. They are often used synonymously but there are important differences.

> **EXAMPLE**
>
> When catching a ball a child must execute the following movements:
>
> ■ Move the hands to an interception position.
> ■ Close the fingers at the right time

In order to perform the movements in the example he/she will also need to have/be aware of:

■ A sense of position in relation to the ball (spatial visualisation).
■ The parabolic flight path of a ball.
■ The time it will take for the ball to reach the hands (velocity and acceleration prediction).
■ Personal reaction time.

Perceptual-motor abilities

A study by the National Aeronautics and Space Administration in the United States (Parker *et al*. 1965), measured the primary dimensions of perceptual-motor performance appropriate for the Gemini space mission. Eighteen basic perceptual-motor abilities were identified and classified into four categories:

19

Fine manipulative abilities

- *Arm/hand steadiness*. Hold hand and arm steady when fully extended.
- *Wrist/finger speed*. Make rapid repetitive tapping movements.
- *Finger dexterity*. Manipulate small objects with fingers.
- *Manual dexterity*. Manipulate large objects with hand.

Gross positioning and movement abilities

- *Position estimation*. Reaching for specific locations without use of vision.
- *Response orientation*. Make appropriate directional response to non-spatial stimulus.
- *Control precision*. Make fine, controlled positioning movements.
- *Speed of arm movement*. Make discrete, rapid arm movements.
- *Multi-limb co-ordination*. Use hands and/or feet simultaneously.
- *Position reproduction*. Repeat discrete arm–hand movement without aid of vision.

System equalisation abilities

- *Movement analysis*. Differentiate target velocity and acceleration.
- *Movement prediction*. Integrate target motion components to estimate future target position.
- *Rate control*. Control vehicle having first-order system dynamics.
- *Acceleration control*. Control vehicle having second-order system dynamics.

Perceptual-cognitive abilities

- *Perceptual speed*. Make rapid visual comparisons of display elements.
- *Time sharing*. Divide attention among several displays.
- *Reaction time*. Respond as rapidly as possible to discrete signal.
- *Mirror tracing*. Use mirror-image display to perform directional hand–arm movements.

Fleishman (1964) stated that the differences between 'skill' and 'abilities' are as follows:

The term 'skill' refers to the level of proficiency on a specific task or a limited group of tasks. . . . When we talk about proficiency in flying an aeroplane, in operating a machine lathe, or in playing basketball, we are talking about a specific skill . . .

The assumption is that the skills involved in complex activities can be described in terms of more basic abilities. For example, the level of performance a man can attain on a machine lathe may depend on his basic abilities of manual dexterity and motor co-ordination. However, these same abilities may be important to proficiency in other skills as well.

FIGURE 5 Skill in sport: a combination of innate ability and acquired skill

Definition of ability

'Ability' refers to a more general trait of the individual, which has been inferred from consistencies in response for certain kinds of movements. These are fairly enduring traits that in the adult are more difficult to change. Many of these abilities can be seen as a result of learning and can be developed at different rates. (Adapted from Fleishman 1964.)

Psychomotor ability

The ability to process information that relates to movement and to turn resultant decisions into action.

Psychomotor abilities include reaction time and limb co-ordination.

Gross motor ability

Ability involving actual movement, e.g. strength, flexibility, speed. (Adapted from Honeybourne *et al.* 2000.)

Fleishman et al. (1964) developed a 'taxonomy of human perceptual motor abilities'. The results were based on perceptual motor tests given to many different people. Following these experiments Fleishman identified eleven measurable perceptual motor abilities. He also identified nine abilities that he categorised as physical proficiency abilities. These are sometimes known as gross motor abilities:

Perceptual motor abilities: Fleishman's categories

1　Multi-limb co-ordination, e.g. the co-ordination of arms and legs in the high jump.
2　Control precision, e.g. the fine-tuning of muscular actions in a snooker shot.
3　Response orientation, e.g. quick decision making about the type of pass to be made in hockey.
4　Reaction time, e.g. processing information quickly to choose a shot in cricket.
5　Speed of arm movement, e.g. moving the arm rapidly in the javelin throw.
6　Rate control, e.g. – change speed and direction accurately to track the target in clay pigeon shooting.
7　Manual dexterity, e.g. well directed arm–hand movements in catching a frisbee.
8　Finger dexterity, e.g. finger control in darts throwing.
9　Arm–hand steadiness, e.g. precise arm–hand movement in crown green bowls.
10　Wrist, finger speed, e.g. wrist/finger speed in spin bowling.
11　Aiming, e.g. in archery.

Physical proficiency abilities (gross motor abilities)

1　Static strength – prop forward in rugby.
2　Dynamic strength – press-ups.
3　Explosive strength – long-jump take-off.
4　Trunk strength – strength of trunk muscles used in gymnastics.
5　Extent flexibility – flexing and stretching back muscles in trampolining.
6　Dynamic flexibility – repeated trunk flexing movements in toe touching.
7　Gross body co-ordination – co-ordination of several parts of the body in motion, as in bowling in cricket.
8　Gross body equilibrium – maintaining balance without visual cues in a rugby scrum.
9　Stamina – capacity to sustain maximum effort in a marathon race.

The above are examples identified by Fleishman but there are probably many others that could be considered, including dynamic and static balance, visual acuity and tracking, eye–hand co-ordination.

There are also intellectual abilities to be considered such as memory capabilities, speed/accuracy in making perceptions and solving problems. All these can be important in the performance of motor skills in sport.

These abilities are related to performance in a variety of basic movements in sport and will differ from one individual to another.

A classification of abilities such as the one above is useful in the identification of common characteristics of related groups of abilities. This commonality can then be used in the selection of performers who have the required groups of abilities as well as in identifying those ability groups that need to be nurtured and/or developed at an early age.

One of Fleishman's key points in his definition of ability was:

a more general trait of the individual which has been inferred from certain response consistencies on certain kinds of task.

There has been controversy in relation to the concept of 'general motor ability' that some authorities believe can actually be measured. There is, however, a more recent and general agreement that such abilities are specific rather than general.

A successful sports performer has many highly developed basic abilities and may be proficient in a great variety of specific tasks. These tasks related to sports performance can share common abilities.

Many sports psychologists support the theory of specificity in motor abilities and this view is supported by research that has shown that the relationship between any two abilities (e.g. reaction time and balance) is low.

Singer (1966) also demonstrated that the relationship between the two fundamental motor skills of throwing and kicking was very low.

The 'all round' sportsperson can therefore be seen as possessing numerous abilities that can be applied to the movement being attempted at any one time. Hand–eye co-ordination, which is so important in tennis, can therefore be applied or transferred to table tennis. This is often referred to as *skill transfer*.

The abilities that contribute to performance early in the learning process in some skills (the cognitive stage of learning) are not necessarily the same abilities that will contribute to later more advanced performance.

Fleishman (1967) comments:

> **Abilities can be thought of as capacities for utilising different kinds of information. Thus, individuals who are especially good at utilising certain types of spatial information make rapid progress in the early stages of learning certain kinds of motor tasks, whilst individuals who are more sensitive to proprioceptive cues do better in tasks requiring precise motor control.**

When considering the acquisition of motor skills in sport it is important to take into account the contribution made by specific activities to the development of abilities rather than just the teaching of specific skills dependent upon such abilities. As we know, abilities are largely genetically determined but they can be nurtured and modified, particularly in early childhood.

Whereas this may make intuitive sense, most agree that abilities are the foundation stones of skill learning and it is on these abilities rather than advanced skills that initial teaching should be concentrated. Whichever view is subscribed to it is vitally important that young children are given the stimuli of movement experience.

These early experiences will enable children to develop both physically and cognitively and will hopefully motivate them to learn more about sports performance. It is therefore vital that those responsible for the teaching of young people during these formative years attempt to cultivate these more general abilities prior to their becoming involved in specific skill learning (or coaching). The emphasis on this development of abilities should be at primary rather than secondary school level and yet, sadly, most of our physical education specialists are to be found in the secondary rather than the primary sector.

Task analysis

The analysis of sports tasks is important so that relevant individual abilities and skills can be recognised. Once these abilities have been identified then the teacher and the learner can strive to develop them. Figure 6 represents a task analysis of the badminton serve. It shows each component of the serve and identifies some of the abilities required for the movement.

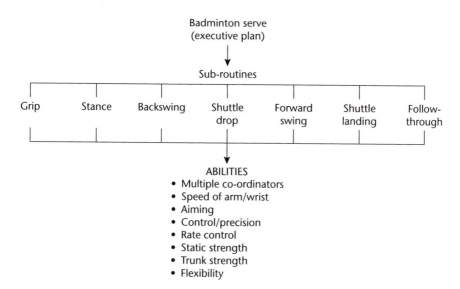

FIGURE 6 Task analysis: a badminton serve

Emotional intelligence

There has been much recent interest in the concept of emotional intelligence and how this can affect behaviour.

The amount of emotional intelligence any individual may have is called the Emotional Intelligence Quotient (EQ). Emotional intelligence is increasingly relevant to both organisational and individual development because the EQ principles provide a new way of understanding and assessing behaviours, attitudes, interpersonal skills and potential.

The EQ concept argues that conventional intelligence (IQ) is too narrow a measurement. Other aspects of our emotions are also important and can influence how successful we are. Success requires more than just IQ – which ignores many other behavioural elements.

Some people are academically brilliant but are socially and interpersonally inept. We also know that success is not automatically conferred upon those with a high IQ rating.

There are two important elements of emotional intelligence:

■ Understanding yourself, your goals, intentions, responses, behaviour and all.
■ Understanding others, and their feelings.

There are said to be five 'domains' for emotional intelligence:

- Know your own emotional behaviour.
- Managing your emotions.
- Motivating yourself to have the most appropriate emotional response.
- Recognising and understanding other people's emotions.
- Managing relationships, e.g. managing the emotions of others.

By developing our emotional intelligence in these areas we can be more successful in acquiring motor skills and help others in their own learning.

The development of emotional intelligence can also reduce levels of stress for individuals and organisations such as football clubs or sports teams, by decreasing conflict and improving relationships.

REVIEW QUESTIONS

CHARACTERISTICS AND CLASSIFICATION OF ABILITIES IN SPORT

1 Give a definition of ability in sport.
2 What are the main differences between skills and abilities in sport?
3 What abilities are used when a child catches a tennis ball?
4 Give examples of gross motor abilities and perceptual abilities in sport.
5 List five abilities identified by Fleishman and give a sporting example for each.
6 What intellectual abilities does a mid-field hockey player require?
7 Why has the concept of a general motor ability been discredited?
8 Explain what is meant by the 'specific abilities hypothesis'.
9 Analyse two tasks in your chosen sport, identifying the abilities that are needed.
10 How can schools help more in the development of abilities related to sport?

Texts referred to in this chapter

Fleishman, E. A. *The Structure and Measurement of Physical Fitness*, Englewood Cliffs NJ, Prentice Hall, 1964.

Fleishman, E. A. 'Individual differences and motor learning', in R. M. Gagne (ed.) *Learning and Individual Differences*, Columbus OH, Merrill, 1967.

Honeybourne, J., Hill, M. and Moors, H. *Advanced Physical Education and Sport*, Cheltenham, Stanley Thornes, 2000.

Parker, J. F. Jr, Reilly, D. E., Dillon, R. F., Andrews, T. G. and Fleishman, E. A. 'Development of tests for measurement of primary perceptual-motor performance', Houston TX, NASA, CR-335. 1965.

Singer, R. 'Comparison of inter-limb skill achievement in performing a motor skill', *Research Quarterly*, 37, 406–10, 1966.

chapter three

INFORMATION PROCESSING IN SPORT

The mind and how it works are still largely a mystery. In sport, skills are learned and performed by making important decisions having sorted out a complex array of information or stimuli.

The brain takes in information from the environment as well as drawing on previous experiences before it sends messages to our muscles to move in a particular way.

With the development of the computer, interest grew in the theories and models that might reveal some of the processes of learning rather than the effects of the environment. Cybernetic or information processing explanations have become a fashionable way of explaining how information is processed so that sports skills can be learned and performed.

Terms in common use in the world of computers – such as 'input', 'central processing', 'output' and 'feedback' – are now commonly used to refer to the human counterparts of senses, the brain, muscular responses, and proprioceptor feedback. Figure 7 is a general, simplified example of a cybernetic model.

FIGURE 7 A simple information-processing model

How movement is controlled

Cybernetic theory, including feedback as closed-loop control via the servomechanisms (proprioceptors) of the body, has stimulated research into how movement is controlled. There are numerous models and explanations that stem from information processing theory.

The reception, transformation, and storage of information by the individual, together with decision-making functions and perception, selective attention, memory, speed of processing and decision making, are all of central interest to researchers who wish to understand how the brain processes information related to the learning and performance of motor skills.

Welford (1960) recognised three primary systems: (1) perceptual mechanisms, (2) translatory mechanisms, (3) effector mechanisms. Whiting (1975) went on to develop a more complex model – see Figure 8.

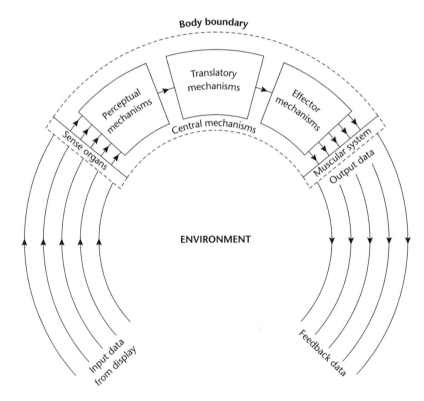

FIGURE 8 Systems analysis of perceptual motor performance (Whiting 1975)

Perceptual mechanisms

The perceptual mechanisms register the incoming information in the brain.

> **EXAMPLE**
>
> The retina in a goalkeeper's eyes would register the image of a football coming towards him.

Translatory mechanisms

The translatory or decision-making mechanisms interpret the information and form a motor plan for an appropriate response. Following on from the example above, the goalkeeper judges the speed and direction of the ball and decides to dive quickly to the left.

Effector mechanisms

The effector mechanisms relay the movement decisions to the muscular system. So, having realised that the ball is coming towards him, and deciding that it is moving to his left, the goalkeeper dives to the left with outstretched arms.

Sensory input

Just as information goes into a computer to be processed, stimuli enter the brain to be considered before action. This is called sensory input.

We take in information (stimuli) via our sense organs, the three most important being: (1) vision, (2) audition, (3) proprioception.

Vision

The eyes receive light waves, which are converted to electrical impulses and these impulses are transmitted to the brain. In sport vision gives us some very important information about the movement of objects and other people in the environment, as well as our own position in relation to these things.

Audition

The ears receive information via sound waves, which are also converted into electrical impulses and passed to the brain. The perceptual process then interprets this information, so that the goalkeeper hears the shout of a team-mate to take the ball – followed by the welcome sound of the ball thumping into his gloves.

Proprioception

This is the information that is received about the body's position and movement. This information is intrinsic and arises from nerve endings called proprioceptors, found in the muscles, joints and the inner ear. Proprioception is often referred to as *kinaesthesis*.

When information enters the brain it is encoded as the brain recognises just what the stimulus means. Memory plays a crucial part in this recognition process, as it is – at least in part – the result of previous experiences that are stored there.

The short-term sensory stores filter information or stimuli – a process called *selective attention*.

EXAMPLE

The goalkeeper may receive information such as crowd noise and movements/shouts of other players that is not required in order to make a save. More experienced goalkeepers, will be accustomed to 'selecting out', filtering and ignoring irrelevant information.

The capacity for any player to attend to information is limited. Therefore it is crucial to select what is important in that snapshot of time. The more tired the player the more limited is the capacity to attend to information, and the more skilful a player the greater the attentional capacity Kahneman (1973).

Factors that affect selective attention include:

- *Relevance*. The goalkeeper may judge that the striker's foot is more relevant than the waving of the crowd.
- *Expectation*. The goalkeeper expects there to be a shot because of the body position of the striker.
- *Vividness*. The loud shout by a fellow player is more likely to be attended to than a passing comment from another.

There are thought to be stores for visual and auditory information (*visual store* and *auditory store*) but these stores hold information only very briefly – this is thought to be less than one second.

The stimuli that are selected as being important pass through the short-term memory store and are organised into manageable 'chunks'. Information can also be passed into the long-term memory if it is repeated and is sufficiently important.

The role of memory in information processing

Most psychologists regard memory as a process rather than an entity. This process is admirably illustrated by the information-processing model (refer to Figure 7). The brain is viewed as actively altering and organising information rather than merely recording it. There are three stages of remembering information according to the information processing approach: (1) encoding, (2) storage, (3) retrieval.

Stages of remembering

Encoding

Involves the conversion of information into codes. These are known as:

- Visual codes.
- Auditory codes.
- Semantic codes.

Semantic codes refer to the storage of information according to its meaning. If a basketball coach outlines a tactical play we may not remember it word for word, but we will remember the essential meaning that is conveyed.

There are forms of encoding related to the motor programme approach discussed in Chapter 4, which codes particular movements such as riding a bicycle.

Storage

This concerns the retention of information over a period of time.

Retrieval

Involves recovering the stored information and its success depends on how well known the information is and how much there is of it.

Multi-store memory

The information processing approach to memory includes the *multi-store memory model* (Atkinson and Shiffrin (1968)), according to which there are three stores: (1) short-term sensory store (STSS), (2) short-term memory store (STM), (3) long-term memory store (LTM).

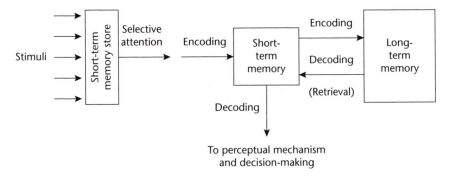

FIGURE 9 Multi-store memory model (after Atkinson and Shiffrin 1968)

Short-term sensory store (STSS)

Filters information/stimuli by means of the process known as selective attention.

Short-term memory (STM)

Information that has been filtered and attended to is passed into the STM, which can retain information that is presented immediately for about twenty to thirty seconds. Information that has been rehearsed will be retained for longer.

EXAMPLE

A netball player can rehearse the coach's pre-game instructions by repeating them to herself several times.

Many authorities agree that the STM can only hold between five and nine pieces of information, although its capacity can be increased through the organisation of the information. This is known as *chunking*. It is thought that when the STM is full, new information replaces the old.

Long-term memory (LTM)

Information that is rehearsed sufficiently over a period of time in the STM is passed to the LTM, which is thought to have an unlimited capacity for holding information for an indefinite period. It is thought that nearly all the information that is forgotten is the result of failure to retrieve rather than the memory being wiped out.

PLATE 5 Relevant information about an opponent is stored in the long-term memory

Photo: Tony Marshall/EmPics Sports Photo Agency

Another view of memory

The table tennis player uses both the STM and the LTM to perceive what is happening and to make appropriate decisions as a result. In order to hit the ball there is constant referral to what is already known (LTM) and what is about to happen (STM). Baddeley (1986) called the STM the 'working memory' because of the amount of information going back and forth between it and the LTM. According to Baddeley, there are three components of the working memory:

- *The rehearsal loop*. This is the STM in Atkinson's model. When the netball player is rehearsing her coach's instructions.
- *The visuo-spatial sketchpad*. This allows the temporary holding of a visual image. For example, the netball player will visualise a particular attacking move.
- *The executive control system*. This controls the amount of information that may be judged at any one time, as decisions are made. The player may consider two or three possible moves before selecting the one she feels will be the most successful.

Yet another view of memory!

Research shows that memory is dependent upon the depth of processing. (Craik and Lockhart 1972.)

This view disputes the multi-store model and suggests that there is an initial analysis of information in what is called the *primary memory* by a *limited-capacity central processor*. This processor identifies the type of information entering the brain and then uses an appropriate method to remember it.

For example, if a basketball player is trying to remember an offensive play during a match, he may talk through the series of numbers repeatedly to himself. If the player is trying to make sense of his coach's instructions he may deal with it semantically – in other words, by trying to understand what is being said.

The processing of this information in the primary memory results in the creation of a *memory trace* and the effectiveness of this memory trace depends on the depth of processing that takes place. The more meaningful the information then the deeper the processing of that information will be. Hence it is more likely that any information will be remembered.

The levels of processing theory would support the view that someone who is learning a sequence of gymnastic skills, for instance, will remember more effectively if they practise it physically and take more time over understanding the nature of each movement required in the sequence.

Increasing the effectiveness of memory

There are a number of ways in which we can make our memory processes more effective. This will help significantly in optimising sports performance.

Rehearsal

This can be useful for retrieval of information in both the STM and the LTM.

The coach will encourage the tennis player before she serves to go though the action mentally in her head and the possible reactions of her opponent.

Meaningfulness

The more the information is seen as relevant to our needs the more likely we are to remember it.

The tennis coach will show that the coaching information that is being given will raise the performances level of the player.

Association

If new information is linked with old information it is more likely to be remembered, thus associating it with something already known.

> **EXAMPLE**
>
> The tennis coach will show the player that new information regarding the serve technique is simply an adaptation of the old serve, so that the learning of a whole new skill is not required.

Avoiding overload

Any new information must be allowed to 'sink in', thus avoiding potential confusion.

> **EXAMPLE**
>
> The tennis coach will give the player only a few points to remember before the match.

Organise information

We have seen that 'chunking' can expand the STM store. Complex pieces of information should be grouped in order to aid understanding.

> **EXAMPLE**
>
> The trampolinist will remember a complex sequence by mentally putting the small moves together to build more difficult ones.

Mental imagery

Linked with the above method, a visual representation can often be remembered far more easily than verbal instructions.

EXAMPLE

The trampoline coach demonstrates the move to the performer or shows her a video of the sequence so that it can be remembered more effectively.

Translatory mechanisms

Once the information has been through the perceptual mechanism, the brain then has to formulate a plan regarding the movement that must take place. This is called the translatory mechanism or *decision-making mechanism*. If the performer is receiving a tennis serve, the player has to decide which shot to play, based on the information that has been filtered and influenced by the memory.

Once the decision has been made, messages are passed through the nervous system to the muscles; this is called the *effector mechanism*. The muscles then move as a response and the skill is performed.

The time it takes to make a decision when performing in sport is critical. If too much time is spent weighing up a situation any advantage over an opponent can be lost. It is therefore important that decision-making time or *reaction time* is kept to a minimum.

EXAMPLES

A sprinter must react quickly to the stimulus of the gun to get the fastest possible start.

A netball player must react quickly to mark an opposing player who has moved into space.

A squash player must react quickly when the opponent plays a drop shot rather than a drive.

Reaction time

The following terms are used when considering reaction time:

- *Reaction time*. The time between the presentation of a stimulus to the very start of the movement in response (e.g. the sprinter hears the gun and makes a decision to drive off the blocks).
- *Movement time*. This is the time between the start and the finish of a movement (e.g. the sprinter drives off the blocks, runs the race and finishes).
- *Response time*. The time between the presentation of a stimulus to completion of the movement (reaction time + movement time) (e.g. the time between the sprinter hearing the gun to the finish of the race).

Factors affecting reaction time

In order for a performer or a coach to improve reaction time it is important that the factors that affect the ability to react quickly are identified.

Hick's law (see Figure 10) states that the greater the number of choices that have to be made, the longer it takes to react. If there is only one stimulus and one

PLATE 6 Reaction time is all-important here

Photo: Photodisk

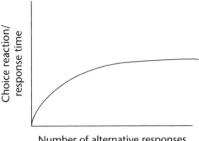

FIGURE 10 Hick's law   Number of alternative responses

possible response, it is known as *simple reaction time*. If there is more than one stimulus and more than one response, then this is known as *choice reaction time*.

Hick's law

Choice reaction time is linearly related to the amount of information that must be processed for the required response to be activated (Honeybourne *et al.*, 2000). In other words the more alternatives you have to choose from, the longer your reaction time will be.

EXAMPLE

In a badminton game, the larger number of possible shots that you have, the slower the opponent will be in their response to your shot.

The age of the performer

As the performer matures and becomes more experienced reactions are quicker but they also slow down with age.

Previous experience

The more experienced the performer the more likely it is that he/she is able to anticipate a number of responses. Practice in reacting to expected stimuli in sport can enable an habitual response. This is sometimes referred to as *automaticity*.

The psychological refractory period

The above term is applied to the period of time that it takes for one stimulus to be recognised and cleared before a second stimulus can be dealt with. This causes a delay in response and is caused by the brain being unable to process more than a single item of information at any one time. This is known as the *single channel hypothesis*. This states that, when receiving external stimuli, the brain can deal with only one stimulus at a time. It is also often referred to as the *bottleneck theory*.

EXAMPLE

Performing a 'dummy' is a typical way of delaying an opponent's tackle in rugby. The opponent has to clear the initial decision to tackle before responding to the new stimuli. This can gain valuable time for the player performing the dummy.

Stimulus–response compatibility

If the response is normally associated with a particular stimulus (e.g. the sound of gun to drive off the blocks in a sprint race) the response is faster.

Feedback

Following the completion of a motor skill, there is often information that we recognise which can inform us about how well (or poorly) we have performed. This process is called *feedback* and helps us to know what to do in similar

---

EXAMPLE

A novice gymnast might not be aware of what a headstand feels like. Therefore, feedback on the performance given by the coach would help to detect and correct errors. The coach might use video to help identify strengths and weaknesses.

---

circumstances in the future. The coach or teacher must give appropriate feedback to a novice performer because he or she may not be able to detect their own errors due to their limited kinaesthetic sense.

Feedback involves using the information that is available to the performer during or after the performance of a skill. There are several forms of feedback:

- *Knowledge of results (KR)*. This is terminal feedback that informs the performer about the end result of their actions.
- *Knowledge of performance (KP)*. This is information about how well the movement is being executed, rather than its end result.
- *Continuous feedback*. This is intrinsic feedback occurring during the performance. (Known as kinaesthesis or proprioception.)
- *Terminal feedback*. Feedback obtained after completion of the response.
- *External/extrinsic/feedback*. This arises from external sources, for example, from what we see and hear.
- *Internal/intrinsic feedback*. This is continuous feedback that is relayed via the proprioceptors.
- *Positive feedback*. This often takes the form of praise and reinforces skill learning.
- *Negative feedback*. This involves information about incorrect movements. This can ensure that the incorrect movement is not repeated.

Effective feedback

Often the effectiveness of information processing depends on the quality and nature of feedback. The type of feedback that is given or that is available to the novice is different to that available for the more experienced sports performer. The novice will not have intrinsic feedback that can be accurately relied upon because of his/her lack of experience and kinaesthetic awareness.

> **EXAMPLE**
>
> A young child who has never played tennis before is given a racket and asked to hit the ball. The child cannot judge (intrinsically) whether the shot has been made using the correct technique.

More experienced performers will have built up a store of previous experiences that can be used to judge the present performance – see Chapter 4 on motor programme theory.

Any feedback that is given should involve the following:

- *A limited amount of information*. There is a danger of overloading the performer with information, especially the novice. There should also be a focus on very specific, easily understood points.
- *Should be immediate*. The feedback should be given as soon as possible after the performance so that the performer can relate the information to very recent personal experiences that have recently been retained in the memory store.
- *Related to the individual*. Sometimes team feedback is important because of the need to review tactics collectively and co-ordinate play but the most effective feedback is directed at specific individuals. They can then relate to the feedback more readily and are accountable in future actions.
- *Facilitate intrinsic feedback/kinaesthesis*. This encourages performers to recognise for themselves the quality of their movements and enables them to correct errors almost immediately.

EXAMPLE

When coaching the forward roll in gymnastics, effective feedback would include encouraging the performer to recognise the feel of the correct movement so that changes can be made during the performance.

- *Positive rather than negative* (most of the time). This is much more motivating and leads to a pleasant learning environment that encourages rather than discourages. Praise must be earned however, because otherwise it becomes devalued. Negative feedback is valuable at times but must always include suggestions on how to improve, rather than unqualified criticism.

INFORMATION PROCESSING IN SPORT

1 Draw and explain the basic model of information processing.
2 What are the three main receptors of information when acquiring skills in sport?
3 What is selective attention and where does it take place in the memory process?
4 What factors affect the ability to attend selectively?
5 Explain the three memory stores according to the multi-store model of memory.
6 Give examples from sport showing how information is retained in the long-term memory.
7 Define reaction time, movement time and response time. Give an example from sport for each.
8 Identify five factors that affect the speed of response in sport.
9 Why is feedback important in acquiring motor skills in sport?
10 Give suggestions about how to make feedback effective when teaching motor skills.

Texts referred to in this chapter

Atkinson, R. C. and Shiffrin, R. M. 'Human memory: A proposed system and its control processes', in P. Scott et al. Psychology, Oxford, Blackwell, 1968.

Baddeley, A. Working Memory, Oxford, Oxford University Press, 1986.

Craik, F. I. M. and Lockhart, R. S. 'Levels of processing: a framework for memory research', Journal of Verbal Learning and Verbal Behaviour, 11, 671–84, 1972.

Honeybourne, J., Hill, J. and Moors, H. Advanced PE and Sport, Cheltenham, Thornes, 2000.

Kahneman, D. Attention and Effort, Englewood Cliffs NJ, Prentice Hall, 1973.

Welford, A. T. 'The measurement of sensory-motor performance: survey and reappraisal of twelve years' progress', Ergonomics, 3, 189–230, 1960.

Whiting, H. T. A. Concepts in Skill Learning, London, Lepus Books, 1975.

chapter four

MOTOR PROGRAMMES AND MOTOR CONTROL

The information processing approach, explained in Chapter 3 shows that the functions of the brain can be explained using the analogy of a computer. This makes it easier to understand more clearly the processes that take place when we are learning and performing skills.

This analogy can be extended to explain how we successfully make so many quick and decisive movements in sport with little time for careful consideration. The theory that seeks to explain this is called the *motor programme theory*.

The plan of action that has been formulated in the decision-making stage of information processing (see Chapter 3) has then to be organised so that commands can be sent to the muscular system. The set of movements that is put into action is stored in the long-term memory and is known as a motor programme or an *executive programme*.

A motor programme is a generalised series of sub-routines that are stored and triggered by making one decision. Once they have been thoroughly learned these motor programmes can become *sub-routines* of more complex programmes. There is therefore a hierarchy of motor programmes.

> **EXAMPLE**
>
> A basketball dribble can be learned so that it becomes a motor programme – almost an automatic response. The player does not have to think consciously about the dribbling action.

Once learned, this programme can become a sub-routine of a higher-order skill such as the lay-up shot.

A motor programme can be stored only if there has been a considerable amount of previous experience – such as the basketball player who has dribbled the basketball thousands of times.

A novice dribbling the basketball has to attend to every aspect of the movement but the expert does not have to concentrate as much because it occurs as a flowing and almost natural action.

The motor programme theory is often referred to as *open loop control* and forms the first part of Marteniuk's theory of motor control.

It is called 'open loop' because any available feedback cannot be acted upon in such a short time. This is particularly evident in ballistic or 'reflex' movements such as a goalkeeper's save or a volley at the net in tennis.

Definitions:

> **a set of muscle commands that are structured before a movement sequence begins, and that allows the entire sequence to be carried out uninfluenced by peripheral feedback . . .**
>
> *Keele (1968)*

or:

> **a motor programme is 'generalised' and controls a 'class of actions'.**
>
> *Schmidt (1988)*

Motor control

According to Martenuik, the level of control attained by the performer dictates the degree of influence of the central nervous system on the control of a motor skill. His view is that the more the skill is learned the less reference is made to feedback information. The first level of control described below is much more relevant to the highly skilled performer than the novice.

Level 1

At this level movements have become almost automatic and reactions are so quick that there is little time or need to act on feedback available. The motor programme activates the muscles to move in a particular way and is so well rehearsed that it can cause actions to take place that are nearly always exactly the same. There are very few attentional demands. At this level the sports performer can attend to other peripheral stimuli whilst performing the motor programme.

> **EXAMPLE**
>
> The motor programme of the basketball dribble is so well learned that the player pays little attention to the action of dribbling. The attention of the player is broadened and allows the movement of other players to be taken into account.

Level 2

The muscular system receives proprioceptive stimuli, which provide feedback. This produces what is known as *closed loop control*. The 'loop' is closed because any intrinsic feedback is absorbed quickly and unconsciously.

> **EXAMPLE**
>
> A gymnast on a balance beam retains balance because the proprioceptors pick up information that is fed back, enabling small movements to correct any errors in balance.

Level 3

This level involves more conscious control by the brain. There is feedback as in level 2 but at this level the muscles and the brain are stimulated with information about the movement. This process takes more time because the brain evaluates

PLATE 7 Immediate absorption of feedback allows instant adjustment

Photo: Photodisk

the movements that are taking place and this can cause loss of important time in making a further response. Co-ordination can also suffer because some of the decisions made by the brain may be incorrect, especially with a novice.

EXAMPLE

A novice trampolinist may perform part of a simple routine incorrectly and have to start the move again. This is because control has been lost and feedback, from both muscles and the brain, has recognised that the fault cannot be remedied immediately.

Closed loop theory

This theory was proposed by Adams (1971). He asserts that movements are initiated by:

acquiring skill in sport

- The *memory trace*. This enables the appropriate response to be recalled from the long-term memory store. The response has been stored because it has previously been a successful response. This memory trace is the 'open loop' element of this theory and was described by Adams as a 'modest motor programme'.
- The *perceptual trace* which controls the movement once it has been initiated by the memory trace. The perceptual trace is developed from experiences with various sources of feedback.

According to the 'closed loop' theory, when someone is practising a motor skill they are continuously matching the perceptual trace with feedback. If feedback tells the performer that the movement matches the perceptual trace, then the movement continues. Conversely, if the feedback informs the performer that there is something wrong because the movement does not match the perceptual trace, then the action is corrected. This process can happen throughout the movement and errors are continuously detected and corrected.

EXAMPLE

In tennis a forehand shot may be instigated by the memory trace, which recognises the situation and chooses the appropriate response.

Once the shot begins, the perceptual trace takes over and controls the fine adjustments that must take place for the shot to be effective. As the arm swings through, the perceptual trace maintains its influence and the shot is adapted according to the flight of the ball, which may perhaps deviate because of spin.

A golfer driving off the tee can sense whether the swing is effective during the action and feedback is received internally. This may be acted upon and the golfer may alter the action during the swing. Some golfers do not need to look where the ball is going because they have 'sensed' the effectiveness of the swing and can visualise the resulting shot. The loop is closed because feedback is present and is acted upon. (Modified from Honeybourne 2003.)

Implications of the programme theory

Many movements in sport are made quickly so that, if a motor programme can be formed for a particular action, reaction time is likely to be short. There is time to adjust movements if the situation changes and attention can be directed to include other aspects of the environment.

EXAMPLE

A hockey player dribbling the ball does not have to concentrate on the skill but can assess a range of possible passes.

Practice plays an important part in the formation of motor programmes. Repeated practice will ensure that there is little conscious control needed in the game situation.

A programme is more likely to be formed if the movements are meaningful to the performer, so the coach needs to make practices relevant and emphasise their importance in the competitive situation.

The internal feedback received is crucial for closed loop control. If coaching practices are as close to real game situations as possible then the internal feedback experienced in training becomes relevant and useful in the game situation.

Schema theory

Schmidt (1975) recognised that there were some fundamental flaws in Adams's closed loop theory.

- There are many different movements possible when performing any skill, so that thousands of memory traces would need to be available. This would put an enormous burden on the performer's memory capacity.
- The closed loop theory also relies heavily on feedback (which is not always used) and that almost automatic movements are very common in sport, e.g. the goalkeeper's 'reflex' save.
- Movements in sport are sometimes completely novel and unique. This also does not agree with Adams's theory, which stresses that for every movement there is a memory trace.

The consensus view is that motor programmes are more generalised than Adams hypothesised. He viewed them as being much more specific.

Schmidt proposed a model of learning that involved 'schema'. According to this theory the sportsperson does not store very specific copies of movements but ideas of relationships or schemes that can be used to adapt the motor programme response to specific situations.

These relationships between muscular proprioception and actual responses are stored after they have been experienced. The long-term memory stores these schemes, which do not include *all* memories of previous actions, just their essential elements.

This theory suggests that the performer stores four items of information in the memory after each movement:

■ *Knowledge of initial conditions*. This includes the position of the body and aspects of the environment.

> **EXAMPLE**
>
> A netball shooter will take into consideration the position of her feet, her body, how far away she is from the goal and the position of her opponent.

■ *Response specifications*. These are the specific requirements of the skill to be performed at that particular moment. This will have the effect of recalling an appropriate motor programme.

> **EXAMPLE**
>
> The netball shooter will 'tell herself' what actions need to take place, including the appropriate technique, the required pace of the ball and the angle of the shot.

The previously learned movements that have been stored as a motor programme in her long-term memory will be recalled.

- *Sensory consequences*. These are the feelings associated with the movement that are recorded in the memory when putting the skill into action. The performer remembers the proprioception or kinaesthesis both during and immediately after the action.

EXAMPLE

The netball shooter is aware of the ball leaving her hands at a particular angle and speed. Intrinsic feedback also informs her of the position of her body.

- *Response outcomes*. This is information about the end result of the movement or action compared with the expected outcome. The performer notes whether the action has been successful or unsuccessful.

EXAMPLE

The netball shooter is aware of what should happen when she shoots and takes note of whether the shot was successful or otherwise.

These schemes form an abstract set of rules. The response requirements of a novel situation, for example, can be related to these general rules. The more general movement schemes that are available the more likely it is that the performer will be able to adapt to different situations.

Experiencing movements in a variety of situations generates a wide range of schemas. This makes *varied* practice very important. If practice conditions are too similar then this results in the creation of schema that are limited in their scope. The use of many different practice conditions can cause a wide variety of schemes to be formed.

Schema are developed effectively through variable practice. Research shows that with two groups of learners,

- Group A, a constant practice group, practising a single element of a skill,

- Group B, a variable practice group, practising several elements of a skill or task,

both groups practise for the same amount of time.

Group A typically acquires basic skill movements more quickly than group B because the amount of learning needed is minimal. For example, the run-up for the gymnastic vault will be learned more quickly than the run-up, take-off, flight-on, flight-off and landing practice.

When these same subjects are then given a novel task with elements of similarity to the original task, it is group B that outperforms group A. This research evidence has been interpreted to mean that if variable practice is experienced then the experiences gained (schema) can be adapted to novel tasks more readily than those who have had limited experience. Variable practice therefore encourages the ability to 'generalise' – the performer can apply or generalise past experiences to new learning experiences.

Recall schema

This is a term that includes knowledge of initial conditions, response specifications and, to a certain extent, knowledge of results. The recall schema remembers motor programmes that were successful and uses them in future actions.

Recognition schema

Are used to evaluate responses and are developed by using knowledge of initial conditions, sensory consequences and knowledge of results. Using these schemas, the performer can estimate what certain movements will feel and look like, which can then be used to evaluate performance.

Transfer of learning

This occurs when the learning or the performance of one skill influences the learning and performance of another. Where this influence can help to produce skilful movement it is called *positive transfer* but when it hinders learning and performance it is known as *negative transfer*.

The main assumption in most skills practice is that whatever is learned during practice will be beneficial to future performance. Positive transfer takes place in many sports practices. For example, physical training is assumed to make the player fitter for the real game situation.

Techniques used during training are meant to carry over to the skills used in the game. Negative transfer can hinder performance and should therefore be avoided as much as possible.

When a player is good at tennis, for instance, and then attempts to learn badminton, he or she may initially demonstrate incorrect technique because of a failure to allow for the different characteristics of the shuttle and the tennis ball. In such situations, negative influences are often superseded by positive ones.

The design of appropriate practices must take into consideration the need to optimise the effects of positive transfer.

Research has produced differing and sometimes contradictory findings, but there are some points, which can be generalised:

There is only a small amount of positive transfer between two skills unless they are almost identical; then there is a large amount of transfer. The reason for such findings is referred to as the *specificity of skill* hypothesis. This proposes that skills are defined by a profile of abilities and that a person's ability to learn and perform a skill depends upon whether that person possesses the right mix of abilities appropriate to that skill. Skills that are apparently only slightly different (e.g. crawl leg action in the water and on the poolside) may have little effect on each other because the learner may have the abilities necessary for one but not the other.

EXAMPLE

In one study, students learned how to execute a volleyball pass before they learned a basketball tip for accuracy. They also practised a badminton volley before learning a tennis volley. In both cases, learning the first action had little positive value when learning the second. The same occurs when one particular action is used but is practised slowly first and then at normal speed. (Adapted from Sharp 1992.)

The more similarity between skills the larger the amount of transfer. This concept is often referred to as the *identical elements theory* – the greater the number of elements identical between the two skills the greater the amount of transfer.

EXAMPLES

- Front crawl and butterfly arm actions in swimming.
- Environmental cues, such as the way in which a tennis ball or shuttle travels.
- Strategies, such as movement off the ball and zone defence.

When practices are set all relevant aspects should be taken into consideration – not just the performance of the skills. Transfer is also more effective if the performers themselves can identify the transferable elements and understand the nature of transfer, thus making a much more discriminating athlete.

The skill must be thoroughly learned before positive transfer can take place. There needs to be a substantial amount of experience before transfer can take place.

EXAMPLE

A novice golfer must practise the basic swing many, many times before it can be transferred to a number of different situations.

PLATE 8 The swing can be applied/transferred to specific shots

Photo: John Walton/EmPics Sports Photo Agency

Terminology related to transfer

- *Intertask transfer:* the influence of experience with one skill on a new skill.
- *Intratask transfer:* the comparison of different types of practice conditions that may affect the learning of a skill.

acquiring skill in sport

- *Bilateral transfer:* the transfer of learning from one limb to another. Learning can be transferred from one muscle group to another, probably via a generalised motor programme.
- *Proactive transfer:* the influence of one skill on a skill yet to be performed.
- *Retroactive transfer:* the influence of one skill on the learning or performance of a skill that has previously been learned.

EXAMPLES

- The young footballer who is encouraged to kick with his left foot as well as his right.
- The basketball player who should dribble with her right hand as well as her left.

Practice with one limb can improve the performance of the non-practising limb – researchers are unsure why!

MOTOR PROGRAMMES AND MOTOR CONTROL

1. Can you define what is meant by the term 'motor programme' and give a practical example from sport.
2. What is the difference between 'open loop' and 'closed loop' control?
3. Can you explain Marteniuk's levels of control?
4. What are the two important elements of Adams's closed loop theory?
5. Why is Adams's theory sometimes referred to as the open/closed loop theory and what are its limitations?
6. Give three implications for coaching related to the motor programme theory.
7. Giving practical examples for each, give the four items of schema information proposed by Schmidt.
8. Why is varied practice so important in sport?
9. What is meant by negative transfer? Give an example from sport.
10. What guidance would you give a coach to ensure that positive transfer takes place in training?

Texts referred to in this chapter

Adams, J. A. 'Closed loop theory of motor learning', *Journal of Motor Behaviour*, 3, 111–50, 1971.

Honeybourne, J. *BTEC Sport*, Cheltenham, Nelson Thornes, 2003.

Keele, S. W. 'Movement control in skilled motor performance', *Psychological Bulletin*, 70, 387–403, 1968.

Marteniuk, R. G. *Information Processing in Motor Skills*, New York, Holt Rinehart & Winston, 1976.

Schmidt, R. A. 'A schema theory of discrete motor skill learning', *Psychological Review*, 82, 225–60, 1975.

Schmidt, R. A. 'Motor and action perspectives on motor behaviour' (1988), in, R. A. Magill, *Motor Learning*, WCB, Brown & Benchmark, 1993.

Sharp, R. *Acquiring Skill in Sport*, Loughborough, Sports Dynamics, 1992.

chapter five

INDIVIDUAL DIFFERENCES

Motivation

The degree to which a performer is motivated to learn skills is key to effective learning. The performer must value the learning activity to ensure optimum performance.

There is often a feeling of complacency once skills have been learned and this can lead to a plateau (or levelling out) of performance. Motivation is important in sustaining skill-learning habits and the enthusiasm to adapt to changing circumstances and demands.

In order to understand how motivation can affect the learning and performance of motor skills it is important to investigate what is meant by motivation. The following show a good level of agreement:

- 'A drive to fulfil a need' (Gill 1986).
- 'Energization and direction of behaviour' (Roberts 1992).
- 'The internal mechanisms and external stimuli, which arouse and direct our behaviour' (Sage 1974).

Most psychologists agree that motivation is to do with an inner force that encourages and drives us towards a particular behaviour.

EXAMPLE

An athlete may be driven to achieve a personal best in the javelin throw. He is driven by a strong desire to achieve a predetermined goal – to throw further than previous efforts and further than his opponents.

Intrinsic motivation

Intrinsic motivation is the intrinsic drive to participate or to perform well in sport. Intrinsic motives include the emotions of fun and enjoyment and the satisfaction that is experienced by achieving something. One definition of intrinsic motivation is:

> **An inner striving to be competent and self-determining; a sense of mastery over a task and to feel a sense of achievement.**
>
> *(Martens 1987)*

Some athletes describe the intrinsic 'flow' experienced during competition. They speak of high levels of concentration and a feeling that they are in total control. This experience is often called being 'in the zone', a term that is related to being on form and having high levels of intrinsic motivation.

EXAMPLE

Olympic oarsman Matthew Pinsent explained that during the final of the coxless fours at the Sydney Olympics, his team 'were working in the zone, the place where your whole being flows into creating a top class performance. I know the zone exists because I experienced it during the race. It feels like time stands still and despite the effort you feel no pain.'

Extrinsic motivation

This is the drive to achieve a goal that is caused by stimuli that are external or environmental. These stimuli or motives are rewards that can be both tangible and/or intangible.

Extrinsic motivation involves influences external to the performer. The drive to do well in sport could come from the need to please others or to gain material and tangible rewards such as badges, trophies, medals or money. Rewards involving winning or receiving praise from others are known as intangible rewards.

Extrinsic motivation often encourages better performance in sport. The rewards act as 'reinforcers' so that the actions or performances that gained the rewards are more likely to be repeated because further rewards are desired.

PLATE 9 Tangible reward

Photo: Henry Rogers

Extrinsic motivation can also increase levels of intrinsic motivation – often called the 'additive principle'. However, there are some who believe that too many extrinsic rewards can decrease intrinsic motivation. For instance the level of performance of some athletes has been known to decline as soon as they had been signed up to contracts that paid a great deal of money.

The 'hierarchy of needs'

Maslow (1954) states that our desires to fulfil certain needs can be viewed as a hierarchy. (Figure 11.) The basic needs are physiological in nature, such as the needs for food and drink. The highest need in this hierarchy is self-fulfilment or 'self-actualisation'. It is shown that our basic needs must be mostly satisfied for higher needs to be realised. According to Maslow, self-actualisation can be realised only if all other needs have been fulfilled.

In sport there are many opportunities to reach the ultimate level of self-actualisation. Sport can create experiences where there can be a great sense of achievement against all the odds such as in climbing or sailing, when the elements are often conquered and self-doubt is overcome.

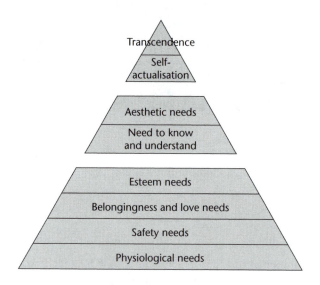

FIGURE 11 Maslow's hierarchy of needs

Arousal

This term is often used to describe and/or measure the levels of an individual's motivation or drive. The amount of drive, alertness or readiness for action is often referred to as the arousal level.

Arousal levels involve both physiological responses – such as heart rate and adrenaline levels in the blood – and psychological responses – such as increased amounts of attention.

The appropriate level of arousal is important for the best performance level both in sporting performance and for optimum learning conditions.

The reticular activating system of the brain regulates intrinsic arousal. External stimuli activate this part of the brain and enable it to adjust to situations that demand a response.

EXAMPLE

When receiving a tennis serve we need to be both physiologically and psychologically alert so that we are ready to respond to a particular stimulus – the tennis ball coming over the net. If we are *too* aroused our performance may suffer because our concentration is affected or because we become over-anxious about our performance.

PLATE 10 A state of physiological and psychological readiness

Photo: Tony Marshall/EmPics Sports Photo Agency

When receiving the serve, the performer's reticular activating system is automatically brought into action.

High arousal levels can be beneficial or detrimental to performance depending on a number of factors. There are a number of theories that explore these factors.

Drive theory

Drive theory states that as the level of arousal increases so does performance. The relationship between *arousal* and *performance* is therefore linear, as illustrated in Figure 12.

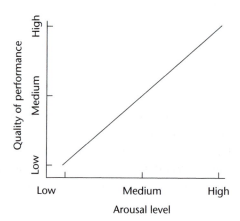

FIGURE 12 Drive theory

Drive theory can be summarised as:

performance = arousal × skill level

If the performer is highly skilled then high arousal caused by a competition or 'match situation' will lead to a high level of performance. If the performer has a low level of skill, then high arousal will lead to a lower level of performance.

There are some criticisms levelled at this theory, because there are many instances in sport where high arousal can be detrimental to performance – however skilled the performer might be. Top athletes are known to have 'frozen' and top golfers have missed relatively simple putts in situations of high arousal.

If a golf shot is learned in a situation where others are watching, this can cause a high level of arousal to be experienced because of the anxiety felt by the learner.

In such a situation the performance often deteriorates because the performer becomes distracted from a task that demands his/her full attention.

If a highly skilled performer is performing a golf shot, the presence of an audience can lead to a high arousal level. In this situation the performance is likely to be enhanced because any distraction caused by the presence of the audience will not affect the performance, which is instigated by motor programmes stored in the long-term memory. (Refer to Chapter 4.)

Inverted U theory

This hypothesis states that an increase in arousal causes an increase in performance but after a certain level, performance then decreases. When represented on a graph this relationship gives the inverted U shape and reveals that the best or optimum level of arousal is a moderate level. (Figure 13.)

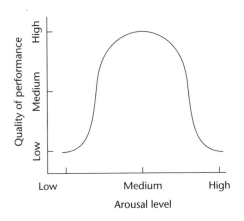

FIGURE 13 The inverted U theory

The level of arousal necessary for optimum performance varies according to three factors: (1) the nature/complexity of the task, (2) the ability/level of the performer, (3) the personality of the performer.

The task

The learning of different types of skill or different types of performance often require quite different levels of arousal. The golfer attempting a putt requires a much lower level of arousal than the weightlifter set to lift a huge weight.

The more complex the skill to be performed the more information has to be processed and the finer the movements that require a calm, measured response. In such a situation, the level of arousal required is low. If the skill is a comparatively simple one requiring dynamic strength and there is little information to process, then a high level of arousal is required for optimum performance. (See Figure 14.)

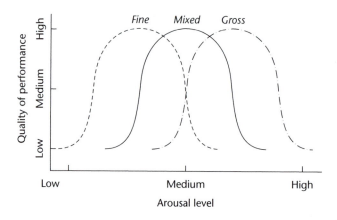

FIGURE 14   Inverted Us, showing different arousal levels for tasks involving 'fine', 'mixed' and 'gross' skills

Tasks in sport, however, are rarely either wholly complex or simple and most sports require a mixture of skill types. A football player may have to make a forceful tackle, which might be immediately followed by the need to make a delicately chipped or precision pass to a team-mate on the move.

The level of ability of the performer

A beginner who is trying to learn a motor skill requires only a low level of arousal. This is thought to be because the learner of a motor skill must fully attend to what is going on and high arousal will distract him or her from that task. (See Figure 15.)

> **EXAMPLE**
>
> The novice will not have stored motor programmes and sub-routines for the most common shots in the LTM. Over-arousal will adversely affect concentration and hamper the player's ability to fully attend to the execution of skills.

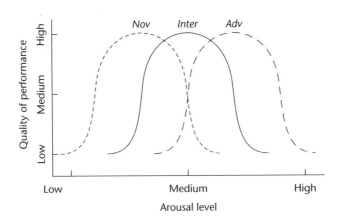

FIGURE 15 Inverted Us, showing different arousal levels for 'novice', 'intermediate' and 'advanced' levels of ability

However, a performer who has reached the autonomous phase of learning and who can draw on a range of well learned motor programmes needs higher levels of arousal in order to produce optimal performance. This is thought to be because higher levels of arousal will increase levels of determination and concentration on stimuli (e.g. tactical implications) that are peripheral to the execution of the skill but which could aid performance.

The personality of the performer

The reticular activating system, described earlier, regulates the amount of arousal experienced by the brain. The type of personality affects the amount of arousal needed by the brain.

Extroverts, whose characteristics include the need to affiliate to other people and social situations, prefer high arousal because there are comparatively low levels of activation by the reticular activating system. High-arousal situations are stimulating to extroverts and enable them to drive towards their goals. Introverts, who do not seek socially interactive situations, prefer low-arousal conditions because their levels of internal arousal are comparatively high and they do not require the extra external stimuli for drive or motivation. (Figure 16.)

EXAMPLE

A netball player who is an introvert may play very poorly in the presence of spectators because she does not seek or enjoy additional external stimulation.

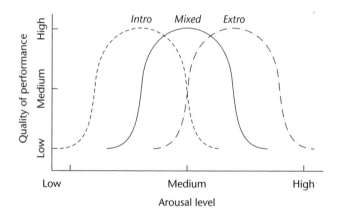

FIGURE 16 Inverted Us, showing different arousal levels for 'introvert', 'mixed' and 'extrovert' personalities

Catastrophe theory

Psychologists have their doubts about the validity of the inverted U theory because many sportsmen and women do not show a steady increase in performance related to arousal and then a steady decrease when arousal is high. There is often a dramatic decrease in performance, which is catastrophic in its effect.

EXAMPLE

The top golfer who misses a simple putt or the professional footballer who misses a penalty.

Fazey and Hardy (1988) suggest that somatic and cognitive anxiety interact to affect performance. When a performer has high levels of cognitive state anxiety ('I am likely to miss this penalty') but has low somatic anxiety ('my body seems to be relaxed and calm'), then performance will be enhanced.

When a performer has high levels of cognitive state anxiety and high levels of somatic anxiety then performance will dramatically decrease. When this 'catastrophe' occurs and eventually arousal is lowered, performance will not return to its previous level until physiological arousal becomes lower than the point at which the catastrophe occurred.

EXAMPLE

A golfer has a simple putt to win or lose a tournament. Both physiological and psychological arousal levels are high. He is so worried that he is unable to control his anxiety and misses the putt.

Figure 17 shows the relationship between arousal level and performance, producing the 'catastrophe' effect:

A   Cognitive and somatic anxieties are both very high and produce a catastrophic effect.
B   Arousal can continue to be extreme . . .
C   . . . and causes even lower performance.

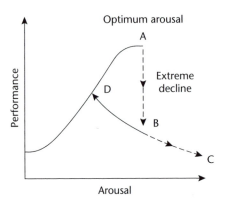

FIGURE 17 Catastrophe theory (Fazey and Hardy 1988)

D   Arousal can be brought under control and as it decreases, performance again increases . . . but does not immediately return to its optimum level.

Personality

Personality characteristics can affect the learning of motor skills in sport. We have already investigated the link between such characteristics and arousal levels, along with the role of the reticular activating system. Personality variables and sports performance are difficult to link and often a piece of research linking a particular type of personality with sports performance is disputed by another.

A definition of personality could be:

> **The sum total of an individual's characteristics that make him unique.**
> *Hollander (1971)*

or:

> **Personality represents those characteristics of the person that account for consistent patterns of behaviour.**
> *Pervin (1993)*

Personality profiles

Sports psychologists have attempted to show that there are major differences between successful sportspeople and those who are unsuccessful or avoid sport.

Morgan (1980) found that successful athletes had positive mental health characteristics. He investigated performers from different sports using a questionnaire assessing their moods – the Profile of Mood States (POMS). Successful athletes were found to have scored higher on positive moods and lower on negative moods. Successful athletes showed high vigour and low fatigue moods. This gave a high point to the profile of the graph, causing it to be known as an 'iceberg profile'. (Figure 18.)

Trait theory of personality

This theory states that we are born with personality characteristics that influence the way in which we behave in sport or in everyday life. Personality traits are stable and therefore vary little over time. Some sports performers may have an aggressive trait and this may surface in a variety of different situations.

Eysenck (1963) saw personalities in two dimensions or scales (Figure 19). These traits should be viewed on a continuum. An individual's personality may have some degree of both introversion and extroversion, with one being slightly dominant.

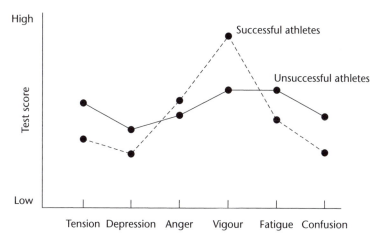

FIGURE 18 An 'iceberg' profile

Extroversion ←——→ Introversion

Stable ←——→ Neurotic

FIGURE 19 Eysenck's dimensions of personality

Team players have been shown to be more anxious and extroverted but lack sensitivity and imagination associated with individual sports performers. (Schurr *et al.*, 1977.)

This type of research should be viewed with caution because there are too many intervening variables present, which makes the link between personality type and performance very difficult.

EXAMPLE

An individual may exhibit behaviour that is sometimes extroverted and sometimes introverted but may predominantly tend to be extroverted.

- *Extrovert*. Seeks social situations and likes excitement. Lacks concentration.
- *Introvert*. Does not seek social situations and likes peace and quiet. Good at concentrating.
- *Stable*. Does not swing from one emotion to another.
- *Neurotic*. Highly anxious and has unpredictable emotions.

The 'narrow band' approach is another trait perspective to personality, which groups personality characteristics into two types:

- A Individuals who lack both patience and tolerance. They have high levels of personal anxiety.
- B More relaxed and more tolerant. They have much lower personal anxiety levels.

Because an individual's personality can also vary during his/her lifetime the trait approach can be criticised as being too unrealistic. Personality characteristics can be affected by different situations.

A hockey player may show signs of aggression only when her team is losing. She is normally a calm and collected individual but losing seems to trigger off an aggressive characteristic.

Research has shown that there is a link between certain personality traits and the sports in which individuals choose to participate but there is little evidence to support the view that the trait approach can predict performance.

Social learning

The social learning approach shows personalities as a group of characteristics that are learned rather than are predetermined genetically. Reactions to situations in sport are often based on how others have reacted in similar situations. We are influenced by 'others' and imitate those who are of 'higher status' than we are. Those other people who influence us in this way are often referred to as 'significant others'. Famous sports personalities are therefore more likely to be copied because they are looked up to and revered by those who are impressed by or aspire to their status.

A young girl who plays for her school team watches a top league netball player being aggressive. The girl will recognise the high status of the player and will wish to copy her behaviour.

Social learning theory suggests that the girl will imitate the aggression because of the high degree of influence of the netball player to her as a role model.

Social learning involves the influences of others on a person's behaviour. We observe and imitate role models but only those who are significant to us.

It is, however, important that coaches and teachers take into account the different motives, levels of arousal and personality characteristics of each individual in their charge order to get the most from them.

Personality tests have been used for selection of sports performers, but these are notoriously inconsistent in their predictions and lack reliability and validity.

Methods of personality measurement

There are many methods of assessing the personality of an individual. The methods used for personality research have problems with reliability and validity. Reliable research achieves consistency of results after two or more applications of tests.

There are two types of validity:

- *Internal validity* assesses whether the research measures what it is supposed to measure. The research instrument or method must be scientific and unwanted variables that are peripheral (nuisance or confounding variables) are kept to a minimum.
- *External validity* assesses whether the results of the research can be generalised to the population as a whole. If the sample used is not representative, then the research has low external validity.

In general terms, laboratory experiments tend to have much lower external validity value than field experiments that are carried out in real-life situations.

Interviews

This method seeks to assess the personalities by discussion. Projective measures, such as the Rorschach inkblot test, have been popular with psychoanalytical theorists. In this test the subject is presented with an inkblot and is asked to describe the 'picture' and what it represents. The responses are then analysed. For example, intelligence is associated with the use of the whole blot and obstinacy is thought to be associated with use of the white space.

Early in the twentieth century, Freud's ideas about the unconscious led to methods of measurement that were based on the premise that individuals will reveal their personality characteristics under the appropriate conditions. According to this approach, if the subject is given ambiguous stimuli, he or she will be caught off guard and will reveal their true self.

Questionnaires

These are sometimes referred to as objective psychological inventories. The use of questionnaires is the most common way of assessing personality. The most common questionnaires used for sports personality research are *Cattell's 16PF* and *Spielberger's Sport Competition Anxiety Test* (SCAT).

Observing behaviour

The subject is watched and behaviour characteristics are recorded. The validity of this method can be very low. If the subject is aware that they are being observed then that in itself will cause behaviour to be modified.

The researcher may also be too subjective in analysing what is observed. What one person reads into a situation may be completely different from another researcher's assessment of the same situation. Observation of behaviour can, however, be valuable in conjunction with other research instruments.

REVIEW QUESTIONS

INDIVIDUAL DIFFERENCES

1 Give a definition of motivation related to sport.
2 Using a practical example, explain what is meant by intrinsic motivation.
3 What is meant by being 'in the zone' in sport?
4 What problems are caused by too much use of extrinsic rewards?
5 Give two examples of extrinsic rewards in sport that are often used to motivate a beginner to learn new skills.
6 Explain drive theory and give an example from sport to illustrate it.
7 Using examples from sport, illustrate the inverted U theory
8 What are the important elements of catastrophe theory?
9 Describe a personality profile that could be used in sport.
10 What are the main differences between trait and social learning theories of personality?

Texts referred to in this chapter

Eysenck, H. J. 'Biological basis of personality', *Nature*, 199, 1031–4, 1963.

Fazey, J. and Hardy, L. *The Inverted U Hypothesis: a Catastrophe for Sport Psychology*? British Association of Sports Sciences, Leeds, National Coaching Foundation, 1988.

Gill, D. L. *Psychological Dynamics of Sport*, Champagne IL, Human Kinetics, 1986.

Hollander, E. R. *Principles and Methods of Social Psychology*, 2nd edn, New York, Oxford, Oxford University Press, 1971.

Martens, R. 'Science, knowledge and sport psychology', *Sports Psychologist*, 1, 1, 29–55, 1987.

Maslow, A. *Motivation and Personality*, New York, Harper and Row, 1954.

Morgan, W. P. *Sport Personology*, Ithaca, NY, Mouvement, 1980.

Pervin, L. *Personality Theory and Research*, New York, Wiley, 1993.

Roberts, G. C. (ed.) *Motivation in Sport and Exercise*, Champagne IL, Human Kinetics, 1992.

Sage, G. H. *Sport and American Society*, Reading MA, Addison-Wesley, 1974.

Schurr K. T., Ashley, M. A. and Joy, K. L. 'A multivariate analysis of athlete characteristics', *Multivariate Experimental Clinical Research*, 3, 53–68, 1977.

chapter six

THEORIES OF LEARNING

Learning has been defined in a number of ways but the overriding view is that experience gives us knowledge and this knowledge in turn directs our behaviour. We learn skills related to sport in the following ways:

- By making associations between stimuli and responses.
- By practising or rehearsing actions.
- By observing others and then copying them.
- By using experiences to gain insight.

These views are explored in this chapter and are related to sports situations.

The associationist view of learning

The term 'associationist' is given to theories related to the bonding of a particular stimulus and a particular response. These are often referred to as S–R theories. We can become conditioned by stimuli that are connected or associated with certain responses.

Classical conditioning

In classical conditioning an existing S–R association gives way to a newly learned bond. Pavlov's experiments with dogs show that the repeated pairing of an unconditioned stimulus with a conditioned stimulus can result in a conditioned response. Pavlov gave food as an unconditioned/natural stimulus to dogs and the dogs' unconditioned/natural response was to salivate. Pavlov then rang a bell at the same time as presenting the food. The dogs salivated because the food was present, but were unconsciously associating or connecting the arrival of food with the sound of the bell. As a result of this association, when the bell was rung again, the dogs still salivated even if there was no food. The dogs' natural behaviour had been changed or certainly modified through the association of one stimulus with another. This modification is called *conditioning* or a conditioned reflex.

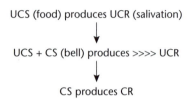

FIGURE 20 Learning by association (Pavlov). *UCS* unconditioned stimulus, *UCR* unconditioned response, *CS* conditioned stimulus, *CR* conditioned response

EXAMPLE

A child is learning to swim but shows fear of the water. The child has already learned the response of fear to the stimulus of the water. If the teacher incorporates fun and enjoyment into the trip to the swimming pool the child's response of fear of the water may change to one which is much more positive.

It is hoped that the child's response would change because the initial fear of the water has been replaced with a response of enjoyment. This would be because the stimulus of the water has become associated with the stimulus of having fun.

Classical conditioning can also be seen in operation when teaching motor skills. The use of repetitive skill drills encourages movements to become almost habitual. The responses of the learner will become classically conditioned when associated with a particular stimulus.

A possible problem with the 'drill' style of teaching motor skills is that the performer may not gain an understanding of why he or she is doing something. This lack of understanding can limit both the extent of learning and the development of further more complex skills.

acquiring skill in sport

A basketball player dribbling the ball sees a route opening up to the basket and drives into that opening to take a shot at the basket in an almost automatic response.

The response above will have been practised many times in training when the stimulus of the opening becomes apparent in a range of situations.

Conditioning is more likely to occur if there is to be minimum punishment and maximum reward. This is often referred to as the cost–benefit analysis.

If a classically conditioned response ceases, it is called *extinction*. This usually occurs when the conditioned stimulus is continually present without the unconditioned stimulus. If the unconditioned stimulus is brought back, even for a short time, the conditioning can be reformed.

It is therefore important, for example, that if you wish a novice swimmer to keep enjoying the water, fun needs to be a regular feature of their visits to the pool.

When there is a stimulus present that is similar to, but not the same as, the conditioned stimulus, the conditioned response can occur. Pavlov's dogs, for instance, salivated after any bell noise, not just the one that was used in the experiment. This phenomenon is called *generalisation*.

The basketball player may, whilst dribbling the ball, drive into any space that presents itself – whether or not it leads to the basket. The response has become generalised to a number of similar stimuli.

If the unconditioned stimulus is presented with only one specific conditioned stimulus, then the opposite of generalisation occurs. This is called *discrimination*.

Pavlov's dogs would show discrimination if they received food only when one particular type of bell rang. They would salivate only when one specific bell sound was heard. In sport the batsman would only play one particular shot if the ball bounced in front of him in one specific way. The cricketer had learned to discriminate one specific stimulus or bounce to generate one specific response or shot.

This is particularly relevant in cricket, where the ability of a batsman to respond appropriately (play the correct shot) to a number of possible stimuli (types of bowling) will determine how long he/she will stay at the crease.

Operant conditioning

Thorndike worked with animals to observe their behaviour and to try to understand the behaviour of humans. He used kittens and placed them in his 'puzzle box'. This was in fact a small cage that had a piece of string attached to its door. The kitten tugged on the rope by accident and the door would open. Each trial increased the likelihood of the kitten opening the door through trial and error. The reward for opening the door was release from confinement.

Thorndike called the principle of learning from trial and error the *law of effect*. He stated that if the consequences of behaviour give satisfaction, then that behaviour would more likely be repeated. If the consequences are unpleasant, then the behaviour is not likely to be repeated.

Thorndike's laws

Thorndike developed a theory based on strengthening the S–R bond. He created 'laws' regarding responses to particular stimuli.

- *Law of exercise*. If the S-R bond is repeated then learning is more likely to take place.
- *Law of effect*. If the response to a certain stimulus produces consequences that are pleasant then that response is more likely with the same stimulus.
- *Law of readiness*. A response is more likely to follow a certain stimulus if the subject is physically and mentally mature and capable enough to carry out that response.

Skinner (1953) continued the work of Thorndike and found that conditioning was more effective by manipulating behaviour towards a stimulus than through modification of the stimulus.

Skinner used apparatus called a 'Skinner's box' with a variety of animals. The animal, for example a rat, would run round the base of the box and would accidentally hit a lever inside the box. This would result in a reward being released in the form of food.

The rat would continue to run round the box but its behaviour would eventually be modified through trial and error and it would simply keep running over the lever and not around the rest of the box. The rat learned that hitting the lever would produce food; therefore its behaviour had been conditioned. This is called *operant conditioning*.

Running over the lever produced food as a reward and this reinforced the action of running. Operant conditioning involves the shaping of behaviour through reinforcement. Unlike classical conditioning, which concerned the modification of the stimulus rather than reinforcing behaviour.

If a reward is always present when behaviour takes place then learning is much faster. This is called *complete reinforcement*.

Research shows that if a reward is given after a number of correct responses learning takes longer but lasts longer. This is known as *partial reinforcement*.

Operant conditioning is widely used in the teaching of motor skills. It is extremely effective.

EXAMPLE

In teaching the tennis serve a large chalk circle might be drawn at the back of the appropriate service box and the learner asked to try to serve into it. After many practice sessions the size of the circle would be gradually reduced and eventually removed, by which time the learner is 'conditioned' to serve accurately.

Rewards are used extensively in the teaching of skills because they reinforce the type of behaviour required.

The above is an example of the *operant* method of conditioning. The target became progressively more demanding and realistic to the 'real' game situation. The correct responses of the learner may have been reinforced by the reward of praise that had shaped his/her behaviour. The actions were also reinforced through the learner's success at hitting the target.

The associationist or *behaviourist* approach to learning has often been criticised because of the lack of realism or *ecological validity*. The experiments that took place were largely set up in laboratories and ignored such variables as whether the natural abilities of the learners might affect the effectiveness with which they learned the connection between a stimulus and a response.

There is also a lack of generalisation – in other words there is the difficulty in linking the behaviour of animals with that of humans. Human behaviour tends to be much more complex than an animal's behaviour. For example, there are motives related to self-fulfilment in humans that is unlikely to be present in an animal's motives for behaviour.

Reinforcement

There are three main types of reinforcement: (1) positive, (2) negative, (3) punishment.

Positive reinforcement

This term refers to the presentation of a stimulus to encourage behaviour that is required to be repeated and therefore to strengthen the S–R bond that is present. The stimulus given is a reward and as such there is a desire to receive more reward and therefore that behaviour will be repeated. Positive reinforcement in the teaching and learning of motor skills can be in a number of forms such as praise from the teacher when the learner makes a required response. There is widespread use of merit badges when certain skills or performances are made.

EXAMPLE

Badges are given when distances are achieved in swimming. Swimming a length of the pool would result in a badge being given to the learner. The learner would experience pride and a sense of success through achieving the distance and might be motivated to swim it again and strive for more rewards for longer distances.

Negative reinforcement

This involves the removal of a stimulus to break a stimulus–response bond.

If a particular behaviour is not the required response, the reward or 'reinforcer' that has been used to encourage that behaviour could be removed – thus discouraging any recurrence of that particular behaviour.

Negative reinforcement is often exemplified by 'avoidance behaviour'. The rat in an animal behaviour experiment may avoid an area of its cage because it will experience an electric shock in that area. Therefore the rat's response of running into that area is weakened but the response of keeping away is weakened. In human motor skill learning the removing of praise may result in an S–R bond being weakened.

If negative feedback or criticism is used when there is an undesired response and then removed when the response is correct, this is also an example of negative reinforcement. Therefore the removal of a certain stimulus can manipulate behaviour by either strengthening a desired S–R bond or weakening an undesired S–R bond.

EXAMPLE

A boy dislikes rugby because he is afraid of pain or embarrassment, which may result in tackling. He will avoid the rugby lessons as much as possible with a note from his parents stating that he is unwell or by avoiding any situation in a game that may involve tackling.

Punishment

This involves the presentation of a stimulus to break the S–R bond. If the response is not desired then punishment can be incorporated.

Punishment becomes linked or associated by the learner with the undesirable response and this response will then be modified in order to avoid future punishments.

In skill learning situations, poor movements might result in negative comments from the teacher. In football a player may receive a yellow card as a punishment or may even be sent off. In many sports players may receive a fine for inappropriate behaviour.

Skinner maintained that positive and negative reinforcement are more effective than punishment in determining behaviour. This is largely because punishment can only make undesirable behaviour less likely rather than encouraging 'desirable' behaviour.

Others have argued that punishment is very effective in modifying behaviour but with humans in particular this can cause detrimental side-effects such as anxiety, lack of motivation and depression.

Some argue that punishment merely suppresses a response rather than a response being unlearned and as soon as the punishment ceases the undesired responses resume. It is likely that a combination of reinforcement and punishment is effective with human behaviour.

Observational learning

Social learning theorists believe that behaviour is learned in social situations and that responses are not simply linked with stimuli in a straightforward S–R approach.

This view considers that there are other variables involved and that learned behaviour arises largely out of the influence of other people.

This approach has grown out of human behaviour research rather than animal behaviour – as is the case in classical and operant conditioning.

Social learning takes place through the observation and copying or imitation of others. The person whose behaviour is being observed is called the *model* and observational learning is often referred to as *modelling*. Responses that develop from observational learning are spontaneous and often there is no intention on the model's part to be teaching any type of behaviour.

Behaviour is more likely to be copied if the consequences of the behaviour both by the model and the observer are desirable. Therefore reinforcement is present but this process is not as mechanical and thoughtless as the conditioning theories.

Reinforcement serves principally as an informative and motivational operation rather than a mechanical response strengthener.

(Bandura, 1973)

Social learning is not just about imitation; it also involves adopting moral judgements and patterns of social behaviour.

In a classic study by Bandura (1973), children watched a display of adult aggression. The children saw an adult attacking a life-size doll. When each child was given a similar opportunity to imitate this behaviour, most of them showed aggressive behaviour similar to what they had observed earlier. There are a number of conclusions that were made arising from such studies:

- If the model shows behaviour that is more *appropriate* according to social norms, it is more likely to be copied. For example aggressive male models are more likely to be copied than aggressive female models.
- The *relevance* of the model's behaviour is important. Boys are more likely to imitate the aggressive model than girls, because boys, through socialising influences, often see aggressive behaviour as appropriate for them.
- Models whose behaviour is reinforced in some way by significant others are likely to be copied.
- More powerful models or those that are perceived to be more powerful are more likely to be imitated.
- If a model's behaviour is consistent, it is more likely to be copied.

Social learning through observation and imitation is very relevant to physical education and sport.

Many of us find ourselves in situations where we can influence the views and behaviour of others, especially children. This may be because we are in a position of authority or because we are good at a particular sport.

Top sports performers sometimes forget that they are avidly watched by many young viewers who will try to copy their every move – they are *role models*, whose behaviour is seen as acceptable and preferable to others.

When teaching skills, it is the demonstration process that is particularly important. According to Bandura (1977), there are five main functions involved in observational learning: (1) paying attention, (2) recording a visual image, (3) retention, (4) motor reproduction, (5) motivation.

Paying attention

To be able to imitate a demonstration, the performer must pay attention to the demonstration and focus on important or pertinent cues. The perceived attractiveness of the model, the competence of the model and the status of the model will influence the amount of attention paid.

The personal characteristics of the observer and the incentives that are present are also important influences. If there are problems in reproducing the learned behaviour, it is often because attention had been distracted or interfered with at the time of modelling.

Recording a visual image

The observer must be able to remember the model that is presented. Therefore he or she needs to create a mental picture of the process. This is often referred to as a *visual image* or a *semantic code*. Mental rehearsal can improve retention of this mental image.

Retention

For this visual image to be stored permanently, there must be rehearsal and good memory organisation.

Motor reproduction

The observer must be physically able to imitate the skill being observed. There must be a number of trials to develop *kinaesthetic awareness* of the skill via intrinsic feedback. In older children, for example, there is more muscular development, therefore it is more likely for the model's behaviour to be copied in more complex actions.

Motivation

The level of motivation of the observer is very important if behaviour is to be observed and copied. External reinforcement of the model will increase the motivation to imitate it, because the perceived consequences will be desirable. (See previous section on reinforcement.)

Demonstrations are very important in the acquisition of new skills. Imitation of the demonstration depends on the observer's attention, visualisation, retention, motor reproduction and motivation.

If a coach or teacher of gymnastics wishes to present/demonstrate a good model of the handstand or use another performer to demonstrate, it would be most effective if:

- The demonstrator/model is successful/significant in status.
- Aspects of the demonstration are highlighted, such as the position of the arms (*attention*).
- The demonstration is repeated and the observer's mental picture (*visualisation*) is stored permanently (*retention*).
- The activity is then practised and rehearsed, with support at first (*motor reproduction*).
- Rewards such as praise or badge/award schemes encourage replication of the model and thus skill-learning (*motivation*).

PLATE 11 Demonstrations should be technically and consistently correct

Photo: Photodisk

Socialisation

The process through which children acquire behaviours they need to have as adult citizens. Socialisation is the process of adopting the *norms* and *values* of a culture. Children learn many important responses, including attitudes, values and self-control, via the influence of their parents and other significant people around them.

Socialisation also involves the adoption of morality, which in turn affects the sports performer's behaviour during competition. According to social learning theory we copy the morality of those who are significant to us. This learning from others is thought to be a gradual process and can also influence gender role behaviour. Evidence often shows that boys and girls are treated differently from birth. This socialisation related to gender can affect the individual's choice of sport and also the motivation to acquire skills in a particular sport. The following research reveals the different ways in which boys and girls are treated (adapted from Dwyer and Scampion 1995):

- When parents are asked to describe their newborn infants, sons were considered to be strong, active and well co-ordinated; girls as little, delicate, beautiful and weak. The researchers found the infants to be matched in terms of size, weight and muscle tone so that these descriptions represent the expectations of parents rather than actual differences.
- Fathers are more likely to encourage the cognitive development of their sons and social development in their daughters.
- Parents often encourage aggression in boys but not girls and, if provoked, girls are anxious about appearing aggressive.
- Male characters in the media are typically presented as aggressive, whereas females are passive.

Cognitive theories of learning

Cognitive theories are concerned with thinking and understanding rather than connecting certain stimuli with certain responses – or by merely being motivated to copy others.

Another term used to represent the cognitive theory of learning is *insight learning*. This is because the learner gains insight not through trial and error but through understanding sufficiently to create a mental image of a solution to the 'whole' problem.

acquiring skill in sport

Gestalt theory

The Gestaltists, (a group of early twentieth-century German scientists) used chimpanzees to investigate this concept. These scientists, including Wertheimer, Kohler and Koffka, established many principles or *laws of perception* and extended these laws to provide accounts of learning and problem solving.

In their experiments, a chimpanzee was placed in a cage and a banana was hung from the roof of the cage. The animal could reach the banana only by putting boxes underneath it and standing upon them.

Problem solving of this type is aided if there is some previous experience of similar stimuli, so that chimpanzees with previous experiences of playing with boxes were able to solve the problem much more quickly than those who had not had such previous experiences.

According to cognitive theorists, we are continually receiving information from our surroundings and we work out what has happened by using our previous knowledge (memory) and general understanding (perception).

This cognitive view is often known as *Gestaltist theory*. (The word *Gestalt* means 'entirety' or 'wholeness of form'.)

The Gestaltist view is that we perceive objects as a whole, rather than a collection of parts. It is therefore considered that when learning takes place different aspects of the environment are drawn together in order to solve the problem.

These different aspects, known as intervening variables, are the mental processes that occur between the point at which the stimulus is received and a response is made.

EXAMPLE

The cognitive view directs us to use 'whole practice' rather than 'part practice' in teaching and learning. Accordingly, if we play the game, in order the better to understand what is required, it is more effective than learning skills separately and in isolation from the 'real' environment.

Providing young people with a variety of sporting experiences can also help with learning and motor development because children can draw from these experiences in order to understand a problem and then solve it – thus gaining insight into the learning process.

Cognitive theory could be used as an argument against didactic/command approaches to the teaching of skills because this rigid approach leaves no room for creative responses that can form the basis of learning and adaptation to other situations.

We can relate this type of learning to the acquisition of motor skills. We copy the skills performed by others because we are motivated to achieve success and because of our drive to be accepted by others. The coach or teacher could be viewed as a 'significant other' or role model and is therefore copied.

EXAMPLE

A cricketer who learns to swing the ball by understanding the basic mechanics of bowling is (perhaps unwittingly) utilising cognitive theory. Similarly, a basketball player who has zone defence explained to him would understand when and why to utilise it.

REVIEW QUESTIONS

THEORIES OF LEARNING

1. What is meant by the 'associationist view' of learning?
2. Describe classical conditioning and relate it to learning a motor skill in sport.
3. What is meant by 'generalisation' and 'discrimination' when applied to conditioning?
4. Explain Thorndike's law of effect and how it can be applied to the acquisition of motor skills in sport.
5. Describe an experiment carried out by Skinner and explain how behaviour of the animals involved was modified.
6. Describe a teaching activity which would encourage operant learning.
7. Define: positive reinforcement; negative reinforcement; punishment.
8. Explain, using examples, how motor skills are learned by observing an expert.
9. Describe and explain Bandura's 'model of observational learning'.
10. Using examples from sport, illustrate the cognitive theory of learning.

acquiring skill in sport

Texts referred to in this chapter

Bandura, A. *Aggression: a Social Learning Analysis*, Englewood Cliffs NJ, Prentice Hall, 1973.

Bandura, A. *Social Learning Theory*, Englewood Cliffs NJ, Prentice Hall, 1977.

Dwyer, D. and Scampion, S. *Psychology*, London, Macmillan, 1995.

Skinner, B. F. *Science and Human Behaviour*, London, Macmillan, 1953.

Thorndike, E. L. *Educational Psychology: Briefer Course*, New York, Columbia University Press, 1914.

chapter seven

PHASES OF LEARNING AND LEARNING CURVES

Stages or phases of learning

Fitts (1967) identified different stages or phases in the process of learning. These phases are not by any means the only way of describing the process of learning, but they form a useful basis for discussion. Each stage or phase embraces a different level of understanding.

Phase 1: the cognitive phase

This phase is sometimes called *the plan formation* stage. A great deal of information must be perceived and understood in the cognitive phase. The amount of information available can be too much for some performers, especially those who have little experience in related activities.

Martenuik (1976) has also described the cognitive phase of learning as the third level of motor control (see Chapter 4). This third level of control has a closed loop element, with proprioceptive awareness, but the control of movement is relatively poor for those who are novices.

The cognitive phase is the earliest stage of learning during which the performer tries to understand the requirements of skill production. Trial and error are a feature of this stage of learning in which the beginner experiments and experiences both success and failure.

When successful, the performer's response is reinforced owing to knowledge of successful results or the receipt of feedback and praise from their teacher or coach. Unsuccessful strategies are also very important, because *schema* can be produced that can be referred to during future performances (see Chapter 4).

95

The performer should understand why failure occurred in order to avoid the same experience in the future. Teachers may use demonstrations or other relevant strategies in order to establish understanding. It is important that relevant cues are both highlighted by the teacher and recognised by the performer (see Chapter 6).

EXAMPLE

When a novice tennis player (cognitive phase) needs to perform the serve, the teacher/coach would demonstrate the correct technique and highlight or cue the important movements so that an accurate mental representation or picture is created.

The coach must also ensure that any demonstration and/or verbal guidance is concise and easy to understand at this initial stage of learning.

The interview studies that formed the basis of Fitts's research identified four areas that should be emphasised in order for effective learning to take place:

- Cognitive aspects.
- Perceptual aspects.
- Co-ordination.
- Control of tension.

Each of the three phases of learning includes these four areas of concern.

In the cognitive phase an executive plan is formulated and there may be some intellectualisation or understanding of the skill. This understanding involves the sequencing of each component of the skill – in other words, putting the sub-routines of the skill in the right order. In a push pass in hockey, for example, the correct grip and initial backward weight distribution occurs before the push action on the ball.

The teacher or coach can use methods that encourage a range of responses:

- *Auditory:* instructions from the coach.
- *Visual:* demonstration or video of the skill.
- *Perceptual:* trial and error.

This will ensure that both *receptor* and *perceptual* mechanisms described in Chapter 3 are used extensively in this phase of learning.

There are, however, a number of factors that limit the capacity of the receptor systems.

Stimulus intensity

If the stimulus stands out against its background then it is more likely to be detected.

> **EXAMPLE**
>
> The use of brightly coloured balls in tennis or cricket may help the novice to hit the ball.

Sensory acuity

The sense organs must themselves be effective if stimuli are to be correctly detected.

> **EXAMPLE**
>
> Performers with poor eyesight may experience delayed learning of the fine motor skills needed in table tennis.

Specificity of detection

This is related to the idea that detection ability is not 'generalisable' or transferable from one context to another. If stimulus detection is very good in one context it does not necessarily mean that this would be the case in other discrimination tasks.

A cricket umpire may be very good at detecting bat/ball contact in the context of a slip catch. This does not however mean that he/she would necessarily be as effective as a slip fielder.

Sources of stimuli

If there are simultaneous stimuli from more than one sensory source then there is a limited capacity for detection.

EXAMPLE

If information comes from both sight and sound the brain can deal with only one piece of information at a time whilst holding the other in the short-term memory.

The theory that underpins this limited capacity is the *single channel hypothesis* described in Chapter 3. The ability to be selective about which stimuli are attended to (selective attention) is crucial if reaction time is to be optimised.

The brain needs to hold on to several signals that may be present when learning and performing skills until they are processed. The period for which a signal can be retained depends on the ability of the performer to divide attention between them. This is known as *time sharing*.

EXAMPLE

A tennis player about to make a service return may have two signals to process:

- The flight of the ball.
- The movement of the server.

> The initial movement of the server is stored briefly whilst the flight of the ball is attended to – showing that both signals share time in the receiver's memory.

The return shot that is played takes into account both the flight of the ball and the movement of the server.

Perceptual capacity

The amount of stimuli that are processed effectively in acquiring motor skills depends upon the efficiency of the perceptual mechanism.

- Perception involves the interpretation of the stimuli or sensory information.
- Perception also involves the *coding* of information so that it makes sense to the performer.

EXAMPLE

A netball player receiving a pass has visual sensory information. As the eyes receive this information it strikes the retinas, causing chemical changes, which in turn create nerve impulses that travel to the brain.

On receipt of a stream of impulses the brain triggers the perceptual process, which is continuous rather than having a definite beginning and end. There is then a procedure by which these impulses are coded or classified and compared with any previously held information. Thus (in very simple terms) the netball player sees a moving object, recognises that (1) it is a netball, and that (2) it must be caught. (Plate 12.)

Individuals can of course 'perceive' or 'recognise' differently. A number of players may interpret the same stimuli in quite different ways. One may see the flight of the ball and perceive that it must be caught, whilst another may move into space away from the ball because she has perceived that someone else will/should catch it. In skill learning different individuals can also interpret a demonstration quite differently.

PLATE 12 What happens next is often determined by previous experience

Photo: Andy Heading/EmPics Sports Photo Agency

EXAMPLE

A hockey coach demonstrating a penalty flick must bear in mind the possibility that one learner may perceive the movement of the body to flick the ball whilst another simply sees a goal being scored.

Look at Figure 21 and describe what you see. If you show it to someone else they may see something entirely different. This is an example of perception being 'individualised'. In teams sports particularly, different players do not always interpret the movement of the ball or of an opponent in the same way.

FIGURE 21 Perceptual confusion: what do you see?

> **EXAMPLE**
>
> A novice basketball player may pay too much attention to the ball and forget to watch the movement of an opponent.
>
> The movement of an opponent may distract a badminton player from watching the movement of the shuttle.

In this first phase of learning it is often difficult for the learner to discriminate between information that is relevant and information that is unimportant to the production of the skill.

In skill learning information that is received but which is *irrelevant* is often referred to as 'noise'. It is therefore important that in this initial phase of learning the performer is helped to attend to the information that is important and to ignore any *irrelevant* information. This process is called *selective attention* (see Chapter 3).

In summary, therefore, the cognitive phase involves the performer learning to *understand* what needs to be done in order to complete the skill successfully. This understanding is dependent on factors related to the perception of incoming stimuli that can be helped or hindered by the quality of demonstrations given by the teacher/coach or 'significant other'.

Phase 2: the associative phase

During this phase of motor learning the performer practises, and compares (or associates), the movements being produced with mental images that will have been created during the cognitive phase and stored in the memory.

Feedback is present and is acted upon and the learner develops an awareness of more complex cues or sets of stimuli.

There is also usually a considerable improvement in performance during this phase of learning. Motor programmes are formed although skills have yet to be fully learned in the sense of becoming 'automatic'.

Fitts (1967) referred to this stage as the *fixation phase*. The amount of practice needed depends upon:

A tennis player in the autonomous phase, serves with more confidence and is able to serve consistently and accurately with the minimum amount of conscious control or thought.

The performer above is able to draw on more sophisticated strategies (such as disguising or putting spin on the serve) and is able to take into consideration peripheral stimuli or cues such as the opponent's position on court.

Learning curves

Motor learning and performance

The terms 'learning' and 'performance' are often referred to as if they are the same but there is an important difference between them.

Learning involves a change in behaviour that is relatively permanent. Knapp refers to 'The more or less permanent change in behaviour that is reflected in a change in performance' (1965).

If a novice basketball player scored one basket out of twenty attempts then clearly only a limited amount of *learning* has taken place. *Performance* on the other hand is a *temporary* measurement of learning and can vary over a period of time.

A single performance is not a complete measure of permanent learning. However, if we review a number of performances produced over a period of time then, taken together, they provide a more accurate assessment of the degree of learning that has taken place. The novice shooting the basketball may in fact produce one very good performance but over an extended period it may be clear that learning is limited.

It is important that progress in performance is analysed if learning is to be effective. The *performance curve* is useful in identifying overall learning.

Note. When plotting graphs to record performance over a number of trials it is usual to record performances (sessions) on the vertical axis and the number of trials (shots) on the horizontal axis.

In this first phase of learning it is often difficult for the learner to discriminate between information that is relevant and information that is unimportant to the production of the skill.

In skill learning information that is received but which is *irrelevant* is often referred to as 'noise'. It is therefore important that in this initial phase of learning the performer is helped to attend to the information that is important and to ignore any *irrelevant* information. This process is called *selective attention* (see Chapter 3).

In summary, therefore, the cognitive phase involves the performer learning to *understand* what needs to be done in order to complete the skill successfully. This understanding is dependent on factors related to the perception of incoming stimuli that can be helped or hindered by the quality of demonstrations given by the teacher/coach or 'significant other'.

Phase 2: the associative phase

During this phase of motor learning the performer practises, and compares (or associates), the movements being produced with mental images that will have been created during the cognitive phase and stored in the memory.

Feedback is present and is acted upon and the learner develops an awareness of more complex cues or sets of stimuli.

There is also usually a considerable improvement in performance during this phase of learning. Motor programmes are formed although skills have yet to be fully learned in the sense of becoming 'automatic'.

Fitts (1967) referred to this stage as the *fixation phase*. The amount of practice needed depends upon:

- The complexity of the skill.
- The motivation of the performer.
- The past experience of the performer.

The associative phase of learning can be related to a second level of motor control, which involves feedback being utilised less consciously and with greater control. (See Chapter 4.)

Timing and control are developed and learned during this phase and the links made between sub-routines. The control necessary for effective skill production is known as *temporal patterning*.

Age also affects learning in this phase, with children being prepared to use 'trial and error' much more readily than adults, who strive for the best achievable results over the shortest possible time.

Demonstrations by the coach, teacher or another performer also take on a different purpose. At this stage of learning a demonstration, instead of giving information as a starting point, will be used to give information that will lead to temporal patterning.

Methods of practice and presentations of skills will be dealt with in the next chapter.

EXAMPLE

A golf coach will draw the learner's attention to other cues that will help in timing and co-ordination. The 'feel' of the swing is important, as well as the rhythm of the stroke and the sound of the club hitting the ball.

The coach may decide to demonstrate an incorrect swing followed by a correct one so that the learner can compare and learn from the comparison.

Feedback is also important in this phase of learning. Self-analysis, although it can be useful, is often difficult to achieve and so the coach or teacher has an important part to play in ensuring that the learner receives appropriate and accurate feedback.

In summary, this is the longest phase and the learner must concentrate on the organisation or temporal patterning of the skill in order to make further progress.

Feedback is crucial in providing the learner with the learner information necessary to improve and to consolidate performance.

Phase 3: the autonomous phase

This is generally regarded as the final phase of the skill learning process and is often referred to as the 'autonomic phase' (Fitts 1967).

When a performer reaches the autonomous stage of learning the motor skills involved are almost automatic and there is very little conscious thought at this first level of motor control. This is essentially open loop control, which does not utilise any feedback that may be available, as it is not required to update the movement. Temporal patterning has been almost perfected and results are consistently correct. It is thought that during this phase the concentration required for the skill to be performed is considerably less than previously required and this allows other peripheral stimuli to be attended to.

EXAMPLE

A basketball player dribbles the ball using little conscious control because the (autonomous) skill is so well established. The dribble may now become a sub-routine of a more complex skill, such as the lay-up shot.

Any distractions that may occur during the performance of an autonomous motor skill are largely ignored and the performer is able to concentrate on more peripheral and complex strategies and tactics.

During this stage motor programmes are completely formed and stored in the long-term memory. Consequently, the time needed by the performer to react or make appropriate decisions is short. Many performers may never reach this stage of skill development: or may reach it in only a limited range of basic/fundamental movements.

If performers are to stay in this phase (retain this high level of skill) they must frequently refer back to the associative phase, where practice helps to reinforce motor programmes.

The performer above is able to draw on more sophisticated strategies (such as disguising or putting spin on the serve) and is able to take into consideration peripheral stimuli or cues such as the opponent's position on court.

Learning curves

Motor learning and performance

The terms 'learning' and 'performance' are often referred to as if they are the same but there is an important difference between them.

Learning involves a change in behaviour that is relatively permanent. Knapp refers to 'The more or less permanent change in behaviour that is reflected in a change in performance' (1965).

If a novice basketball player scored one basket out of twenty attempts then clearly only a limited amount of *learning* has taken place. *Performance* on the other hand is a *temporary* measurement of learning and can vary over a period of time.

A single performance is not a complete measure of permanent learning. However, if we review a number of performances produced over a period of time then, taken together, they provide a more accurate assessment of the degree of learning that has taken place. The novice shooting the basketball may in fact produce one very good performance but over an extended period it may be clear that learning is limited.

It is important that progress in performance is analysed if learning is to be effective. The *performance curve* is useful in identifying overall learning.

Note. When plotting graphs to record performance over a number of trials it is usual to record performances (sessions) on the vertical axis and the number of trials (shots) on the horizontal axis.

A learning curve is a collection of measurements of performance that occur over time. It refers to the relationship between number of trials and levels of performance. This relationship is really a curve of performance but the overall picture of performances gives us an idea of the rate or level of learning.

Performances can vary considerably and graphs showing performances of newly learned skills over time would probably show learning curves that are not a smooth S shape. However, if we ignore the extremes in performances, a smooth S-shaped curve may be more apparent. The more trials that are recorded the more accurate will be the analysis of learning.

Figure 22 represents a typical S-shaped curve showing that there is an initial period when there is little or no learning. The performer may fail completely in the early stages (cognitive phase) of learning a motor skill.

▦   *Point A.* There is a slow rate of initial improvement – when the performer is beginning to learn the skill. The curve at position A is called a *positive acceleration curve*.
▦   *Point B.* There is a sharp increase in performance level over a small period of time – indicated by the number of successful trials. At this point the performer is learning quickly and performance is improving rapidly. This part of the curve is called a *linear curve of learning*, showing a period when there is directly proportional improvement.
▦   *Point C.* There is rather less improvement in performance. The performer may have reached the optimum performance for him/her at that particular point in time. It might be that the performer is simply fatigued or lacks the motivation to improve. This part of the curve is called a *negative curve of learning*.

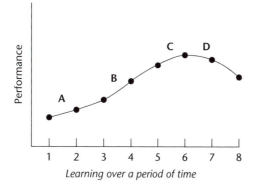

Learning over a period of time

FIGURE 22 S-shape learning curve

- *Point D*. There is no improvement or a decrease in performance. This is called the *plateau effect*. There may well be fluctuations over time at this point but overall there is little or no change in performance. The plateau effect must be combated if performance is to improve.

A performer experiencing 'plateau effect' should:

- Ensure that he/she has enough rest to offset the effects of fatigue.
- Be set goals that are motivating and challenging . . . but *achievable*.
- Increase motivation by varying the content and level of difficulty of each practice session.
- Receive praise and encouragement or little rewards for any achievements.
- Train to improve the physical *and* mental aspects of their fitness.

When coaching or teaching a novice, be aware that there may be times when the rate of improvement will slow down and there may even be a temporary deterioration in the level of performance.

EXAMPLE

After 20 trials a novice basketball player may well be scoring baskets at a lower rate than after 10 trials.

To help address the above:

- Give the novice a rest and reassess the goals, perhaps looking for performance rather than attainment.
- Refer back to technique and ensure there is some success at easier tasks in order to raise confidence.
- Give positive feedback and reward in the form of praise.

Drive reduction

When learning a new motor skill, an individual is often highly motivated to complete a set task in order to achieve skill learning. This motivation is often referred to as 'drive'. When the task is completed (or thought to be completed) the level of this 'drive' or degree of motivation is reduced.

If an individual feels that he or she is performing to the best of his or her ability, then the performance may well become habitual because the performer sees no reason to be motivated or 'driven' to do better.

The level of drive is again reduced if the performer thinks that there is no need to improve further, even though there may in reality be room for much improvement. This is often referred to as *reactive inhibition*.

EXAMPLE

A volleyball player has a high percentage of effective serves. This causes him to stop trying as hard and leads to a subsequent decrease in performance with serves being missed.

The player above has experienced a reduction in his level of drive and his performance has therefore become inhibited.

PHASES OF LEARNING AND LEARNING CURVES

1 What is meant by the cognitive phase of learning? Give the main characteristics of this phase.
2 Why is this phase similar to the third level of motor control?
3 Name the four aspects identified by Fitts that should be emphasised for effective learning.
4 How can stimulus intensity and acuity affect learning?
5 What is meant by 'time sharing' when applied to the processing of information?
6 What is meant by 'noise' when applied to the learning of motor skills and how can selective attention limit its effects?
7 What is temporal patterning in the associative phase of learning?
8 Describe the autonomous phase of learning.
9 Draw an S-shaped performance curve and explain its shape related to the learning of a simple gross motor skill in sport.
10 Identify and explain four practical strategies designed to combat the plateau effect in learning a sports motor skill.

Texts referred to in this chapter

Fitts. P. M. *Human Performance*, San Francisco, Brooks/Cole, 1967.

Knapp, B. *Skill in Sport*, London, Routledge, 1965.

Martenuik, R. G. *Information Processing in Motor Skills*, New York, Holt Rinehart & Winston, 1976.

chapter eight

PRESENTATION OF SKILLS AND PRACTICES

The learning of motor skills is affected by the conditions under which the learning takes place.

There are a number of factors that must be considered before practice sessions are scheduled so that the optimum amount of skill learning can take place. These factors include:

- The portion of the total skill to be practised (presentation of skills).
- The manner in which the practice sessions are spaced in time (presentation of practices).

Presentation of skills

Basic to complex

It is usual to teach basic skills first and then to use these skills as a basis for the learning of more complex ones.

Young children in primary schools are encouraged to participate in basic throwing, catching, kicking and striking activities in order to ensure that fundamental motor skills are thoroughly learned before the more complex sport-specific skills can be learned.

The teaching of sport-related motor skills should involve a progression from these fundamental actions to more complex skills that involve high levels of information processing.

In order to ensure that training practices are helpful, the coach must bear in mind that positive transfer of skills will take place only if the skills being practised are relevant to the real game situation (see Chapter 4 regarding transfer). The amount of positive transfer that can occur will be dependent upon how well previously performed skills have been learned. If a skill is broken down and taught in parts, each part must be learned thoroughly before those parts can be put together and contribute to the whole skill.

Analysis of the task

The nature of the task must be thoroughly analysed in order to identify the important aspects that must be learned and the information that has to be processed.

A *complex* task involves skills that require a great deal of information processing. The perceptual requirements are therefore high and the decision-making process depends on detailed feedback from earlier experiences.

The performer should fully understand the task and therefore careful explanation is needed. The task may be broken down into easier sub-units so that as the performer improves these sub-units can gradually be joined together until the complete task can be performed.

This technique is most effective in learning *open skills* (see Chapter 1) which need high levels of information processing.

The organisation level of the task must also be taken into consideration. A *highly organised* task involves skills that are difficult to split into sub-routines, for example a continuous skill, such as cycling. A skill that has low organisation is easily broken down into its parts or sub-routines, for example the tennis serve.

The presentation of a highly organised skill

Skills that are difficult to split into sub-routines (e.g. cycling) should be practised as a *whole*. Such highly organised skills need to be taught as whole movements because of the difficulty of splitting them into sub-routines. In cycling the use of stabilisers is common as these enable the novice (usually a young child) to experience the action safely. The novice will eventually be able to cycle without the stabilisers; first with manual help, then with very little help and finally with no support at all.

The presentation of a skill with low organisation

These are skills that are easily broken down into sub-routines, for example the tennis serve. This type of skill is best practised by dividing the skill into sub-routines (Figure 23):

1   Preparation of the racket.
2   Swing.
3   Throwing up the ball.
4   Striking the ball with the racket.
5   The follow-through.

Eventually the separate actions can be brought together and practised as a whole.

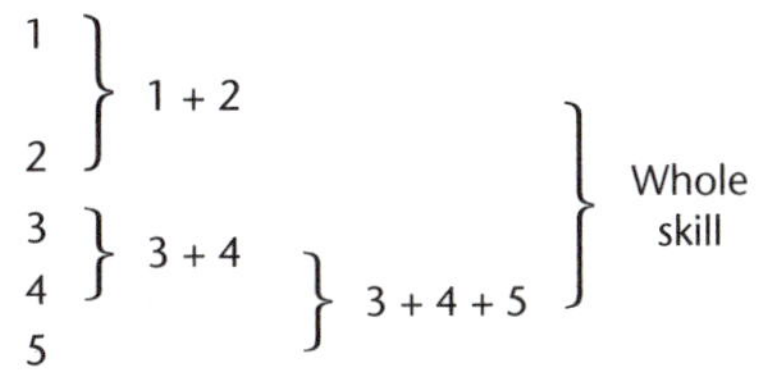

FIGURE 23 Bringing the separate actions together

Teaching skills using the 'part' method

Three different 'part methods' of teaching skills have been identified (Wightman and Lintern 1985):

■   *Fractionisation*. This involves practising the separate sub-routines of the whole skill.

- *Segmentation*. This involves splitting the skill into parts and then practising the parts so that after one part is practised, it is practised with the next part. This is often referred to as the *progressive part* method.
- *Simplification*. Involves reducing the difficulty of the sub-routines of the skill.

Fractionisation

The 'part' method is often used when the skill is low in organisation and can easily be split into sub-routines. If the skill is complex this method is also useful because it allows the performer to understand the requirements of the skill and often achieves early success with basic movements before progressing to the more complex movements.

'Part practice' can also be useful and safe when learning a more dangerous skill, such as those involved in high-board diving, gymnastics or trampolining.

The performer can gain confidence by learning each element of the skill separately and then, when the separate parts are brought together, he/she will have a better idea of the technique involved and be more confident of success.

This form of practice is particularly useful when trying to teach serial skills such as those involved in the triple jump.

The 'part' method of teaching/practice is very useful in working on those aspects of a skill that are giving particular difficulties during performance/competition.

EXAMPLE

A swimmer having problems with breathing during a swimming stroke could practise the breathing/head movement separately using a float.

Segmentation ('progressive part' method)

This is also often referred to as *chaining*. A serial skill is often broken down into its component parts or sub-routines and these can be seen as links of a chain. The performer learns one link and then a second link. The two links are then practised together and then a third link is practised and added to the chain and then further links as necessary until all the links can be practised as a whole.

PLATE 13 Apparently effortless – but only after much practice

Photo: Tony Marshall/EmPics Sports Photo Agency

Coaches and teachers often use a mixture of 'part' and 'whole' methods. The learner develops a picture of the complete movement and begins to understand the relationships between the various components and sub-routines of the whole skill or movement.

This method is very useful in helping the performer to remember the links between sub-routines of skills (see Chapter 3).

EXAMPLE

In breaststroke swimming the leg action is a separate movement from the arm action. There is, however, an important element of timing between the two movements that demands quite complex attention strategies.

If the leg and arm actions are practised independently of each other the attention demands during the learning stages of skill performance are much simpler than if they are learned/practised together.

The two aspects of the stroke can be brought together once they have been learned separately (as parts) so that the learner can then pay particular attention to the strategies involved in timing or synchronising the two actions.

Simplification

Reducing the level of difficulty of the skill is a method that is often utilised in the teaching/learning of more complex skills.

For instance, anyone learning how to juggle would start with larger rather than smaller implements. These are far easier to catch and this allows the learner to pay far more attention to 'timing' than would be possible if early attempts were made with smaller implements. These would be far more difficult to catch and would reduce the attention being paid to 'timing'.

> **EXAMPLE**
>
> Use of a large sponge ball and small plastic racket can help a young child to learn tennis skills. It is far easier to hit the ball with these modified implements so that earlier attention can be given to matters such as the correct placement of the feet.

Teaching skills using the 'whole' method

Here the skill is taught in its entirety without breaking it down into sub-routines. This is usually the best method because the learner experiences the real 'feeling' (*kinaesthesis*) of the skill. The experience can then be transferred as a 'whole' skill from practice to the real 'game' situation.

The performer is much more likely to perform the skill fluently and to appreciate the relationships between each part of the whole movement.

If a task involves a fast or ballistic movement, the 'whole' method of teaching is more effective because the sub-routines of those types of skill are closely associated with one another and are therefore difficult to appreciate when practised separately.

Generally speaking an advanced performer is more likely to benefit from using the 'whole' approach to practising skills in sport. This is because the task can be intellectualised much more easily by a more experienced performer than would be possible for a beginner.

A more experienced performer would also be able to appreciate the links between the various components of the skill without needing to split it into several parts.

It is far more likely that skills presented in such a way (as whole skills) will result
in the formation of well learned motor programmes. This in turn will ensure that
the learner achieves Level 1 motor control and will therefore need to exert less
conscious control over the action. (See Chapter 4.)

In order to determine the best method of presenting skills when teaching motor
skills related to sport, the following factors should be taken into consideration:

- *The experience and nature of the learner*. There may already be some learned
  motor programmes that can be adapted for use. Some learners can cope with
  a great deal of information whilst others cannot. (This can often be linked with
  the age of the learner.)
- *The relationships that exist between the sub-routines or components of the
  skill*. If a skill is continuous, it may not be possible to break it up into meaningful and relevant parts.
- *The coherence of the skill* – if a skill is self-contained and makes sense as a
  whole. In such cases it would be more effective to utilise the 'whole' method
  of learning.

EXAMPLE

Stopping the ball in hockey.

Presentation of practices

The way in which practices that are intended to assist in the learning of sports
skills are set up is important.

For effective skill learning to take place coaches must create the best possible
practice conditions. Variety in training is very important, because it builds up

experiences in the long-term memory as schema (see Chapter 4) and it also makes training more interesting and enjoyable.

Since most participants are to some degree impatient and wish to play the 'full' game or activity whenever they can, training or practice sessions should be as enjoyable and motivating as possible.

For practice conditions to be relevant the following aspects need to be taken into consideration:

- *The type of skills involved*. Complex open skills may need different practice conditions to those that are simple and/or closed.
- *The amount of information to be processed by the performer*. For example, a batsman in cricket has more information to attend to than a sprinter in athletics.
- *Environmental factors*. If the environment were harsh or dangerous, for example, then practice conditions would have to be modified in order to make them relatively safe and secure.
- *The previous experience of the performer*. An experienced athlete may be able to endure harsher and more realistic practice conditions than the raw beginner.
- *The performer's personality and level of motivation*. Many sportspeople are high 'need to achieve' characters. In other words they will always give maximum effort to everything they attempt. Other performers, however, may need different types of stimuli to motivate them to try hard. Some respond to the 'carrot', whilst others respond to the 'stick'.

'Massed' versus 'distributed' practice

The main methods of practice are related to the use of *massed* and *distributed* practice conditions.

Massed practices have fewer sessions but are much longer lasting than distributed sessions. It is a continuous and intensive period of practice. Massed practice may help in the learning of discrete skills that are short in duration.

A: MASSED TRIALS

FIGURE 24 Massed practice: a number of trials with very few rest intervals

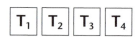

Distributed practice will involve the same amount of practice time but spread over more practice sessions. Consequently each practice session is shorter in duration than massed practice sessions.

Many performers use the intervals between activities to mentally rehearse their skill performances, which can aid the physical performance later.

There is no specific definition of what constitutes massed practice other than the differences stated above.

Research findings tend to favour distributed practice, because massed practice can hinder learning, due largely to fatigue and demotivation.

Distributed practice is best for continuous skills because the player tires easily and allowance must be made for adequate periods of recovery.

Dangerous tasks (for instance those involved in gymnastics) are better trained for using distributed practice. This reduces the likelihood of physical and/or mental fatigue and helps maintain concentration and strength levels.

Gross skills (for example those in cycling and swimming) are more likely to benefit from distributed practice but where the duration of the skill is short – such as the golf drive or the forehand drive in tennis – then massed practice is more likely to be beneficial.

A golf drive and a forehand drive in tennis both involve repetitive/habitual movements. The fluency demanded by these skills is far better attained through repetitive/concentrated practice.

There is of course the danger that too much repetitive practice will cause fatigue and injury and so there must of necessity be an optimum period of time for such practice, depending on the skill involved.

Variety of practice schedules

'Distributed' and 'massed' practice sessions can be constructed in a number of ways. Figures 25–30 represent some of these methods (adapted from Cratty 1973).

B: SPACED TRIALS

FIGURE 25 Distributed practice: a number of trials with relatively long rest intervals (after Cratty 1973)

C: EARLY MASSED TRIALS

FIGURE 26 Massed practice at the beginning of the learning experience (after Cratty 1973)

D: EARLY SPACED TRIALS

FIGURE 27 Spaced practice at the beginning of the learning experience (after Cratty 1973)

E: SPACED/MASSED/SPACED TRIALS

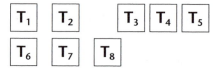

FIGURE 28 Spaced practice interspersed with massed practice (after Cratty 1973)

acquiring skill in sport

F: MASSED/SPACED/MASSED TRIALS

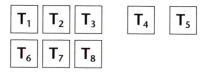

FIGURE 29 Massed practice interspersed with spaced practice to provide rest periods (after Cratty 1973)

G: PRACTICE SESSION

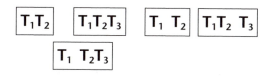

FIGURE 30 Trials arranged so that they correspond to some of the above conditions (after Cratty 1973)

If training lasts for a long period of time, then *inhibition* of the skill learning may take place (see Chapter 7 on reactive inhibition).

This is often caused through lack of motivation or fatigue. Inhibition may also occur if the learner is capable and intelligent and the task presented is too simple. Conversely, inhibition can also occur if the learner is not very capable or intelligent and the task presented is far too complex.

In both of the above instances inhibition can occur because of the difference between the perceived ability of the performer and the perceived difficulty of the task. It is important to recognise that an appropriate activity for one individual or group of individuals may not be appropriate for others.

Variable practice

Practice needs to be varied so that the performer can come into contact with a range of experiences. (See Schmidt's Schema theory in Chapter 4.) Relevant experiences are stored in the long-term memory and these experiences can be used to modify motor programmes in the future.

- In the case of closed skills it is important that practice conditions closely resemble the real game situation.

- In the case of open skills, each situation will be different because conditions are not constant – as in closed skills.

Practice of open skills should therefore be as varied a range of situations as is reasonable. This will allow the performer to store a number of possible strategies for any situation and retrieve them from the long-term memory when needed in competition situations.

This would be particularly important when the skills involved may be rather complex, such as in basketball or hockey.

EXAMPLE

During practice sessions a hockey player experiences a variety of stimuli related to how the ball may be passed to her. If she has been able to stop and control the ball successfully during these sessions the experiences and the techniques involved are more likely to be used in a match situation.

PLATE 14 The player must be able to receive and distribute the ball in any one of a number of ways

Photo: Tony Marshall/EmPics Sports Photo Agency

PRESENTATION OF SKILLS AND PRACTICES

1 What is meant by complexity and organisation in motor skill learning?
2 Describe 'whole' and 'part' methods of teaching skills using practical examples from sport.
3 Explain why you would use the 'part' method, giving a practical example from sport.
4 Describe what is meant by 'fractionisation', 'segmentation' and 'simplification' when learning skills in sport.
5 Explain why you would use the 'whole' method of teaching a motor skill and give a practical example to illustrate your answer.
6 What needs to be taken into account when constructing a practice session for skill learning in sport?
7 Describe the 'massed' and 'distributed' practice methods of teaching motor skills in sport.
8 Draw four simple diagrams to show different combinations of practice conditions.
9 What is meant by *inhibition* in motor skill learning and what causes it?
10 Link *variable practice* with *schema theory* to show how valuable this practice is in the learning of sports' motor skills.

Texts referred to in this chapter

Cratty, B. J. *Teaching Motor Skills*, Englewood Cliffs NJ, Prentice Hall, 1973.
Wightman, D. C. and Lintern, G. 'Part-task training strategies for tracking and manual control', *Human Factors*, 27, 267–83, 1985.

chapter nine

GUIDANCE, TEACHING AND LEARNING STYLES

The amount of learning that takes place when acquiring motor skills in sport is dependent upon the teaching style(s) and methods of guidance adopted by the teacher or coach. These methods must take into consideration the characteristics of the learner including their preferred learning styles.

Teaching and learning styles and their effects on the acquisition of motor skills

There are many different styles that can be used by teachers and coaches. The style or styles that are adopted depends on the following factors:

- The teacher or coach's own characteristics such as personality factors and teaching abilities.
- The type of task or activity that is being taught.
- Factors related to the learning environment.
- The characteristics of the learner, for example, ability level, level of motivation, maturity and their preferred learning style.

If a teaching style is to be effective, then all of the above factors need to be considered.

The characteristics of the teacher or coach

Some teachers or coaches have extrovert personalities and adopt a charismatic style that relies on their persuasive personality. These types of teachers are usually more open and sociable in their approach.

PLATE 15 Genuine or 'for effect'?

Photo: Neal Simpson/EmPics Sports Photo Agency

Teachers who are introverts may use a style which is less teacher-centred and which does not rely too much on personal relationships.

Teachers and coaches who themselves are very capable in the sport being taught may adopt a style that allows them to utilise their own expertise to demonstrate the skills and use a much more 'hands-on' approach.

Teachers and coaches must take account of their own strengths and weaknesses before deciding upon their teaching approach or style.

There are many teachers and coaches who can 'perform' and adopt a role which may modify or be completely different from their own personality.

Mosston's spectrum of teaching styles

In 1986 Mosston and Ashworth identified a range of teaching styles that are defined by the degree of involvement and the proportion of decisions taken by the teacher and the learner(s) respectively as part of the teaching/learning process. (See Figure 31.) This is called the *spectrum of teaching styles*.

When the teacher makes a large proportion of the decisions the teaching style is said to be a 'command' style. When the learner makes nearly all the decisions the style is described as 'discovery'.

The spectrum includes many styles that range between the two extremes of 'command' and 'discovery'.

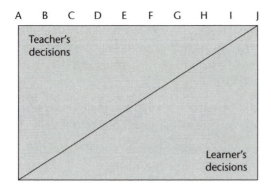

FIGURE 31 The spectrum of teaching styles (after Mosston and Ashworth 1986)

TABLE 1 Advantages and disadvantages of teaching styles

Command style	Reciprocal style	Discovery style
Advantages		
Good for discipline and control	Good for social interaction/responsibility	Encourages individual activity
Good if lack of time	Encourages sense of responsibility	Highly motivating if successful
Good if in a dangerous situation	Develops communication and leadership skills	More personal and relevant information
Good for large groups	Individual/more focused feedback more likely	Easier for teacher but not as much time spent with learner
Disadvantages		
Little social interaction	Learners may not have sufficient maturity	Bad habits/poor strategies could be learned
Little individual involvement in learning	Lack of teacher control	Difficult to unlearn incorrect movements/skills
Lack of creative responses	Incorrect information may be given	A more time-consuming process
Can increase hostility	Lack of status of the pupil Teachers not taken seriously	Could be demotivating if a problem occurs/frustrating

At approximately point C or D in Figure 31 the style is said to be 'reciprocal'. The reciprocal style represents situations when the learners become instructors in the sense that they are able to pass on to their peers the skills shown to them by their teacher or coach. This style also involves the teacher and the pupils, students or performers jointly making decisions.

The 'discovery' method is performer-centred and the learners teach themselves (trial and error) by experimenting with a variety of strategies.

The performers in such cases are usually very self-motivated and have the experience and ability to work without direct help.

Teachers and coaches are wise to adopt a range of styles, depending on the learning factors identified earlier in this chapter. The learner must enjoy the learning experience and should find it possible to experience success; so positive reinforcement is important. (See Chapter 5 on motivation.)

If the teacher has good discipline and the group is large, or if the situation is dangerous, then the command style should be adopted. This style does not allow for interpersonal relationships so there is little interaction or individual involvement in learning.

The reciprocal style of teaching involves more interaction and encourages growth in maturity and communication skills. The discovery style encourages individual creativity but the performer must be well motivated.

Every teacher or coach of skills related to sport should have at their disposal a range of teaching styles. Teachers or coaches should adapt their approach to the type of activity, the age, ability, motivation level and preferred learning styles of the performer. Other factors include environmental considerations and the teacher's own personality and abilities.

The nature of the task

The type of activity being taught also influences the teaching style adopted. If the activity is dangerous, or in a hostile environment, the teacher or coach is more likely to adopt a didactic and authoritarian style so that there is more control over the performer's actions.

The coach must ensure that all the relevant safety factors are understood and adhered to. Allowing learners the freedom to do as they choose at this early stage could result in them putting themselves into personal danger without realising it.

If the skill or activity that is being taught is complex, with high perceptual demands, a style that seeks to explain with detailed instructions might be appropriate. (See Chapter 1 on classification of skills.) The teacher or coach must fully analyse the tasks involved, so that they are in a good position to choose an appropriate teaching style.

Factors related to the environment

Teaching approaches may be affected by the learning situation or environment. Even the weather may dictate the teaching style that is adopted.

Teachers and coaches should assess the environmental situation for each practice session and adopt an appropriate approach.

If there are spectators this may affect the learner's concentration because arousal level may be raised and the learner becomes distracted (see Chapter 5). It is therefore important that the learning environment is as free from distractions as possible.

Characteristics of the learner

The previous experience of the learner must be taken into account before an appropriate strategy for teaching and coaching is adopted.

A beginner may initially find that a more didactic instructional style helps in understanding the requirements of the task. We have seen that during the cognitive phase of learning (Chapter 7) the learner needs to have a clear mental picture of the way in which the skill should be performed. However, if the learner is more experienced a more democratic style allows a greater level of participation. A more experienced individual will be able to make valuable contributions to their own learning, which can be highly motivating because the learner feels more valued.

The motivation levels of the learner can also greatly affect the quality and quantity of learning. If the learner is highly motivated the teacher or coach can concentrate on the requirements of the task without being overly concerned about how to motivate the individual.

Some learners may not be very highly motivated, especially if they feel that their own ability level is greater than the level of the instruction being given. (Figure 32.)

Motivation (see Chapter 5) can also be poor if the learner perceives that they do not have the ability to improve. The appropriate teaching style in such cases should include high levels of positive reinforcement (see Chapter 6) and encouragement.

The age and maturity of the learner must also be taken into consideration:

▪ *Very young* performers need to feel comfortable and safe and therefore a teaching style involving high levels of encouragement should be adopted, with fun activities to maintain levels of motivation and concentration. (Activities that may be perceived as unsafe or very difficult should be presented in ways that minimise the likelihood of this occurring.)

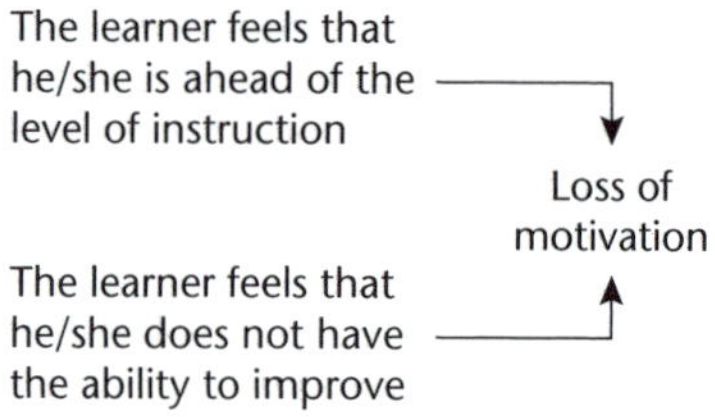

FIGURE 32 Level of instruction can influence motivation

The learner feels that he/she is ahead of the level of instruction ──────┐
                                                                          ▼
                                                                    Loss of motivation
                                                                          ▲
The learner feels that he/she does not have the ability to improve ──────┘

acquiring skill in sport

- *Older* individuals respond better to a more democratic style, which accommodates the views of the learner and gives them more responsibility. (Young or novice performers may not understand some of the language used by the teacher or coach and so the type of instructions given should reflect the age and experience of the learner.)

Learning styles

An understanding of preferred learning styles creates two benefits:

- It helps us understand areas of weakness and gives the learner the opportunity to work on becoming more proficient in the other methods of learning.
- It helps learners to realise their strengths, which can be highly motivating.

Recognition of a range of learning styles also allows teachers and coaches to present sports skills in a way that best suits the needs of the learner (or group of learners in a team situation).

Teachers and coaches are often so concerned with the way *they* present information that they can overlook the performers' need to reflect upon their own learning, which is much more effective for long-term understanding.

David Kolb (1984) developed a 'learning styles' model based on two lines of axis:

- The learner's approach to a *task* (preferring to do or watch). For example, the tennis novice's preference for simply 'having a go' at hitting the ball.
- The learner's *emotional response* (preferring to think or feel). For example the tennis novice's preference for trying to visualise clearly the shot before she attempts it.

The model sets out these four preferences, which are also possible different learning styles:

- *Active experimentation:* doing the activity. 'Learning in this stage takes an active form – experimenting with, influencing or changing situations. You would take a practical approach and be concerned with what really works . . .' (Kolb 1984).
- *Reflective observation:* watching the activity
- *Concrete experience:* feeling the activity
- *Abstract conceptualisation:* thinking about the activity. 'In this stage, learning involves using logic and ideas, rather than feelings to understand problems

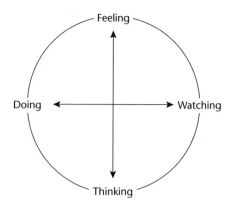

FIGURE 33 Learning style
characteristics (after Kolb 1984)

or situations. Typically, you would rely on systematic planning and develop theories and ideas to solve problems' (Kolb 1984).

These 'learning styles characteristics' are normally shown as two lines of axis. (See Figure 33.)

The horizontal axis is the *processing continuum* (how we approach a task), and the vertical axis is the *perception continuum* (our emotional response).

The combination of these preferences produces four possible learning style types: (1) activist, (2) reflector, (3) theorist, (4) pragmatist.

If the teacher or coach knows the performer's preferred learning style, this enables teaching to be directed in a way that will facilitate the preferred method. Although everyone responds to a greater or lesser degree to all types of learning style, the teacher or coach could emphasise the use of the preferred style where this is possible or appropriate. (Figure 34.)

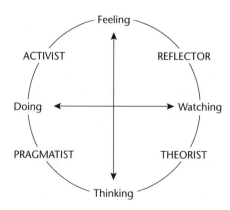

FIGURE 34 Learning styles and
preferences (after Kolb 1984)

■ *The activist:* prefers 'doing and feeling' (concrete-active). This learner prefers a 'hands on' approach and relies on intuition rather than logic. Prefers the practical, experiential approach.

■ *The reflector:* watching and doing (concrete-reflective). This learner is able to look at things from different perspectives, is sensitive and prefers to watch rather than do. This learner gathers information and uses imagination to solve problems.

PLATE 16 Watching others can help beginners develop their own performance

Photo: Photodisk

- *The theorist:* watching and thinking (abstract-reflective). Is concise and uses a logical approach. This learner feels that ideas and concepts are more important than people and also requires a good clear explanation rather than practical opportunities.

EXAMPLE

A volleyball coach gives a clear demonstration of the 'dig' shot and uses verbal instructions to emphasise the coaching points. The practice involves a logical progression of activities.

In the situation above the learner finds that she can build a clear picture of what needs to be done by working out in her mind the requirements of the skill.

- *The pragmatist:* thinking and doing (abstract-active). This learner can solve problems and will find solutions to practical issue dilemmas through the learning experience. This learner prefers technical tasks and is less concerned with people and interpersonal aspects.

EXAMPLE

A basketball coach will encourage the player to find ways of beating a zone defence through training experiences. The player will learn by thinking through the problems as he is playing.

'Theorists' will not be comfortable being given a task without notes and clear instructions. 'Activists' may become frustrated if they are unable to play the game and get practical experiences.

Kolb encouraged the concept of *praxis*, that is:

> **ensuring that opportunities for the interplay between action and reflection are available in a balanced way for students. Praxis means that curricula are not studied in some kind of artificial isolation, but that**

ideas, skills, and insights learned in a classroom are tested and experienced in real life. Essential to praxis is the opportunity to reflect on experience, so that formal study is informed by some appreciation of reality.

EXAMPLE

Kolb's 'praxis' can be applied in a sports context by ensuring that the teaching of motor skills is not isolated from the 'real' game situation and that practice should accommodate the learners' own creativity/thoughts.

The theory of *experiential learning* should always be taken into account in the teaching process. When introducing a new skill the teacher or coach might allow the learner(s) some time to reflect upon what it entails in terms of new or adapted movements and perhaps a further short period in which to discuss it.

Kolb himself points out that the inventory's greatest limitation is that the results are based solely on the way that learners rate themselves. It does not rate learning style preferences through standards or behaviour as some other personal style inventories do. It also gives relative strengths only within the individual learner and not in relation to others.

The wording of some of the questions in the inventory can seem vague to some respondents and the results do not always match the expectations and intuitions of the learner.

Visual, Auditory and Kinaesthetic (VAK) learning styles

Learners have different ways in which they effectively receive and perceive information (see Chapter 3 on information processing, Input). By assessing the learner's style, the teacher can ensure that information is given to them through appropriate methods.

Characteristics of a visual learner

- Best learning takes place when there is a lot of visual input.
- Must have clear demonstrations with cues and without 'visual clutter'.
- Remembers colour, size and location.
- Remembers by clearly visualising or 'photographing' information.
- Learns effectively from videos of their own and others' performances.
- Often have difficulty with verbal instruction.

EXAMPLE

Where a football coach wishes to highlight and change a player's movements on the pitch, he/she could ensure that recent performances are recorded on video-tape and then played back along with feedback about the performance.

Characteristics of an auditory learner

- Learns best by listening to instructions and advice.
- Enjoys discussing problems, tactics and strategies.
- Practices by hearing and recalling.
- Uses sounds and rhythms to remember instructions.
- Is easily distracted by noise.

EXAMPLE

A gymnastic coach gives clear and concise feedback and coaching points immediately after a performance. The feedback is given individually in a quiet room away from distractions.

Characteristics of a kinaesthetic learner

The learner learns best by:

- Actual physical practice.
- Muscle memory so remembers weight and texture.
- Exploring situations by imagining the feelings associated with movements.
- Shadowing the activity through physical movement.
- Likes physical rewards and is tactile.

> **EXAMPLE**
>
> A tennis coach ensures that the learner practises the forehand repeatedly and physically guides them through the correct action.

(See 'Manual guidance' below.)

Guidance in skill acquisition

When a teacher or coach teaches a new skill or strategy to a learner or wants to develop the skills of an experienced performer, the best method to guide the learner must be sought.

There are four main types of guidance that can be used in the teaching and coaching of sports skills: (1) visual, (2) verbal, (3) manual, (4) mechanical. The type of guidance chosen by the teacher or coach, just as the style of teaching, depends upon:

- The personality, motivation and ability of the performer.
- The situation in which learning or development of skills is taking place.
- The nature of the skill being taught or developed.

(Honeybourne *et al.* 2000.)

Visual guidance

This is the most popular and effective method of guidance when used to teach motor skills in sport.

During the cognitive phase of skill learning visual guidance (see Chapter 7) enables the learner to develop a mental image or picture of the skill to be learned. Teachers and coaches often use videos, charts or other visual aids to show the learner a visual representation of a new skill.

Any demonstrations used must be accurate so that the mental image formed by the learner is an accurate one. In order to avoid confusion for the learner there must not be information overload during the early stages of learning. It is important to concentrate on only a few aspects of the performance at a time. The teacher or coach may draw the attention of the learner to a limited number of visual cues so that he/she needs to concentrate only on one or two aspects of the whole movement.

When using visual guidance, it is important for the teacher or coach to ensure that demonstrations are accurate and can be clearly seen by the learner. It is also important that they should be repeated whilst still holding the attention and interest of the performer.

EXAMPLES

- Demonstrations (modelling) of skills by the coach or by another performer.
- Video playback/analysis used to demonstrate and/or highlight strengths and weaknesses in performances.

Verbal guidance

This should be used alongside visual guidance to describe the movement or actions related to the motor skill in question. Verbal guidance has many limitations if used on its own.

There should be a demonstration or other visual representation so that the learner can create the mental image necessary for thorough learning. Verbal guidance can be very effective for advanced performers when more complex information (such as tactics or positional play) needs to be imparted. When using verbal guidance teacher/coaches should:

- *Not* speak for too long. The attention spans of performers are notoriously short in the heat of competition and during/after heavy training.
- Use questioning techniques in order to encourage participation in learning. This can be far more effective than a didactic style.

It is also important to remember that:

- Many sports skills movements cannot be explained satisfactorily without visual guidance.
- Verbal guidance is better used alongside visual guidance in the early stages of learning in order to ensure that the learner has a clear idea of what needs to be done.

EXAMPLES

- Instruction by a tennis coach to a novice on how to grip the racket.
- Calling out cues or coaching points to a trampolinist during a sequence of moves in training.

Manual and mechanical guidance

This may involve the uses of physical support for the learner by another person, using physical guidance and/or a mechanical device.

EXAMPLE

A coach may physically guide novice gymnasts through a vault by supporting their shoulders and guiding them into a safe landing position.

Holding the arms of a golfer and forcing his or her arms through the swing is another example of manual guidance sometimes referred to as a *forced response*.

The use of bicycle stabilisers and a twisting belt in trampolining are forms of mechanical guidance that support a performer and allow potentially dangerous activities to be performed relatively safely.

Manual/mechanical guidance can reduce fear in dangerous situations. The learner will really grow in confidence if they feel safe and it is far more likely that they will attempt the activity without support during the later stages of learning. For instance, wearing armbands will help in learning how to swim. Such methods of guidance and/or support can also allow the learner to experience the kinaesthetic feeling of performing the activity.

EXAMPLES

- A coach supporting a gymnastic move such as the handspring.
- A coach using a support rig in trampolining.

When using manual and/or mechanical guidance, teachers and coaches should ensure that:

- The learner is not given a too unrealistic feeling of the action. The intrinsic feedback received could be incorrect and this may instil bad habits or result in negative transfer. It is advisable, for example, to remove swimming armbands as soon as possible to allow correct stroke technique to be taught and so that a 'real' kinaesthetic sense is experienced.
- The learner participates as fully as possible in order to avoid negative effects upon his/her motivation.

acquiring skill in sport

GUIDANCE, TEACHING AND LEARNING STYLES

1 What factors should be taken into account when considering a style of teaching motor skills?
2 Draw a diagram which represents Mosston's teaching styles.
3 Choose one of Mosston's styles and by using practical examples give the main advantages and disadvantages of using such a style.
4 If the task is dangerous and the environment hostile, which teaching style should be adopted?
5 Using a diagram, describe Kolb's learning styles.
6 What are the drawbacks of using Kolb's learning style inventory?
7 Describe the VAK approach to learning styles.
8 Use practical examples from sport to show how you would teach a skill to a learner who had a predominantly visual learning style.
9 Give practical examples of four types of guidance used in the teaching of motor skills in sport.
10 Give three advantages and three disadvantages of one type of guidance.

Texts referred to in this chapter

Honeybourne, J., Hill, J. and Moors, H, *Advanced PE and Sport*, Cheltenham, Thornes, 2000.
Kolb, D. A. *Experiential Learning*, Englewood Cliffs NJ, Prentice Hall, 1984.
Mosston, M. and Ashworth, S. *Teaching Physical Education*, Columbus OH, Merrill, 1986.

INDEX